T0214975

Azure Kubernetes Services with Microservices

Understanding Its Patterns and Architecture

Kasam Ahmed Shaikh
Shailesh S. Agaskar

Apress®

Azure Kubernetes Services with Microservices: Understanding Its Patterns and Architecture

Kasam Ahmed Shaikh
Kalyan, Maharashtra, India

Shailesh S. Agaskar
Mumbai, India

ISBN-13 (pbk): 978-1-4842-7808-6
https://doi.org/10.1007/978-1-4842-7809-3

ISBN-13 (electronic): 978-1-4842-7809-3

Managing Director, Apress Media LLC: Welmoed Spahr
Acquisitions Editor: Smriti Srivastava
Development Editor: Laura Berendson
Coordinating Editor: Shrikant Vishwakarma
Copyeditor: Kezia Endsley

Cover designed by eStudioCalamar

Cover image designed by Pexels

Distributed to the book trade worldwide by Springer Science+Business Media LLC, 1 New York Plaza, Suite 4600, New York, NY 10004. Phone 1-800-SPRINGER, fax (201) 348-4505, e-mail orders-ny@springer-sbm.com, or visit www.springeronline.com. Apress Media, LLC is a California LLC and the sole member (owner) is Springer Science + Business Media Finance Inc (SSBM Finance Inc). SSBM Finance Inc is a **Delaware** corporation.

For information on translations, please e-mail booktranslations@springernature.com; for reprint, paperback, or audio rights, please e-mail bookpermissions@springernature.com, or visit http://www.apress.com/rights-permissions.

Apress titles may be purchased in bulk for academic, corporate, or promotional use. eBook versions and licenses are also available for most titles. For more information, reference our Print and eBook Bulk Sales web page at http://www.apress.com/bulk-sales.

Any source code or other supplementary material referenced by the author in this book is available to readers on GitHub via the book's product page, located at www.apress.com/978-1-4842-7808-6. For more detailed information, please visit http://www.apress.com/source-code.

Printed on acid-free paper

This book is dedicated to my father, the late Mr. Ahmed Kasam Shaikh, who is always a source of inspiration for me.
And to my mentor, Mr. Sabarinath Iyer.

This book is dedicated to my wife, Mrs. Manisha Agaskar, who has always supported me in all my endeavors.

Table of Contents

About the Authors

Kasam Ahmed Shaikh is an Azure AI enthusiast, published author, global speaker, community MVP, and Microsoft Docs Contributor. He has more than 14 years of experience in the IT industry and is a regular speaker on Azure and AI at various meetups, online communities, and international conferences. He is currently working as Senior Cloud Architect for a multi-national firm, where he leads multiple programs in the Practice for Microsoft Cloud Platform and Low Code. He is also a founder of the community called DearAzure-Azure INDIA (az-India) and leads the community for learning Microsoft Azure. He owns a YouTube channel and website and shares his experience at `https://www.kasamshaikh.com`.

Shailesh S. Agaskar has more than 20 years of experience in information technology. For the last 20 years, he has been working on Microsoft technologies, such as Win32 SDK using C, C++, Office 365, and Azure Data Engineering and Analytics powered by the Azure cloud platform. He has been advising customers across the globe and helping them leverage best-fit technologies to drive their enterprise digital transformation journey. Microsoft platforms and technologies is one of the options heavily leveraged by his customers. He is currently working as Chief Architect for a multi-national firm, where he heads the Practice for Microsoft Cloud Platform, M365, and other technologies.

About the Technical Reviewer

Adwait Churi is a certified Microsoft Azure Solution Architect and MuleSoft Certified Architect and a seasoned professional with more than 12 years of experience. During his information technology career, he has gained experience working in the banking, financial services, and insurance fields, as well as in the LMS (Learning Management System), healthcare, and hospitality domains.

He is passionate about learning new technologies, including cloud, integration, microservices, ETL, and Dev-Ops.

In his day-to-day working life, he helps organizations in software application architecture and designing, pre-sales, performance engineering, project management, and software development. He also provides courses on Microsoft BizTalk Server, MuleSoft, and Microsoft Azure.

Acknowledgments

I would first like to thank Almighty ALLAH, my mother, my better half, and especially my daughter Maryam, for motivating me throughout the process. I am highly thankful to Apress for considering me for this opportunity and for believing in me. Special thanks to Mr. Kishore Chowdary from Team Cloudbeaver for presenting me with Technical help.

CHAPTER 1

Introduction to Microservices and AKS

Introduction

Congratulations, you have taken a step toward understanding microservices better. This book will help you decide when to use microservices and how to solve business problems using microservices. If you are reading this book, you must be interested in designing and developing microservices. Perhaps you are interested in exposing your business to new markets by building external-facing APIs for third parties or perhaps you want to develop and deploy software incrementally and more frequently with agility. Maybe you have no idea what microservices are, but you want to understand this new architectural style that everyone is talking about.

Whatever the reason you're here, this chapter examines what microservices are and why have they become so important and frequently used when modernization is discussed. Microservices are a major step in distributed and service-oriented computing and they have the potential to drastically change the way enterprise-class, large-scale software solutions are developed, today and in the future.

This chapter covers:

- The evolution of software development to distributed computing and how it has evolved into the "software as a service" model.

- What microservices are, when to use them, and why they are useful.

- The benefits realized by microservices style of architecture.

- The principles on which microservices are built.

© Kasam Ahmed Shaikh and Shailesh S. Agaskar 2022
K. Ahmed Shaikh and S. S. Agaskar, *Azure Kubernetes Services with Microservices*,
https://doi.org/10.1007/978-1-4842-7809-3_1

- How microservices are integrated with existing enterprise architectures.

- What the future holds for microservices.

You cannot appreciate microservices without understanding the evolution of the software development world into distributed computing. Therefore, the next section takes a step back in time to see how and where distributed computing began.

The History of Distributed Computing

Stepping back and looking at the history of distributed computing, we can see how microservices are a consequence of a natural evolution. Over time, applications have become more loosely coupled and split into multiple components. This has allowed the distribution of an application across many different machines. This way, multiple computer resources can be used to provide the most resources possible to an application.

The first business use of basic distributed computing involved massive mainframe systems. These expensive computers could handle many users logged into them through dumb terminals, which had no processing power of their own. They simply allowed the users to access resources available on mainframes systems. The only benefit was that these dumb terminals could be located anywhere across the building and could access the central mainframe systems where the processing power and resources were located.

As computers became cheaper and more powerful, it became a viable option to place them on employees' desktops. This changed the way computers were used, because people had access to relatively powerful machines. It made sense to use some of that local processing power, rather than relying on mainframe servers to process every request.

Further evolution of architecture led to the improvements described in the following sections.

Client Server Model

This model involves a central server that contains a database or another central datastore that all clients access (see Figure 1-1). The client handles the user interface screens and some or all of the business logic before sending the data to the server. This frees the server resources so they can focus on processing the data storage. The client machines leverage full resources for everything else and distributes the workload of application across multiple machines, thus reducing dependence on single machine.

- There were major problems with this approach, as maintenance time and new upgrades required shipping new application releases to hundreds or thousands of desktops. They were termed *fat-client applications* and had issues with DLL versioning as managing these became another nightmare. Scaling up these applications as the number of users increased became costly. The resource consumption due to multiple connections increased and made it difficult to increase the number of client machines without increasing the server processing power.

- The solution to this was a new architectural style, after broad acceptance of the World Wide Web. The Web application led to building applications that were accessible through Internet browsers. These applications were called *thin clients* because they used far fewer resources on the client machine. Web applications are deployed on a web server and the business logic is embedded on a separate server. This was the beginning of the Internet and web era, which solved most of the problems described previously.

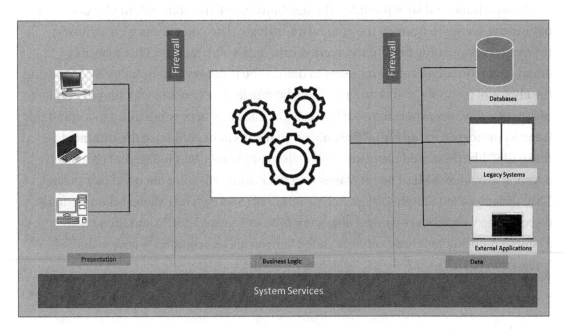

Figure 1-1. *Client server model*

Component Technology

As the client-server revolution was picking up speed, object-oriented programming was picking up steam as well, moving toward a componentized design. A *class* was the minimal unit and the principles of object-oriented programming around it gave rise to designing components and reusing them. This led to the inception of the Component Object Model (COM) and the Distributed Component Object Model (DCOM) in the Microsoft world. In the Java world, Enterprise Java Beans was the answer. The interface contracts were binary contracts. The server side of web applications started to use the component design patterns.

Web Services

Most web applications were now built using a tiered model of the user interface, components, and the database. The components encapsulate the business rules and other specific functionalities as well as access the database. This gave birth to the technology shift/advancement called the *web service*. Web services are fundamentally a distributed solution and their design embraces this by dependence on Internet standards like HTTP and XML.

This architectural style provided the flexibility to use the component object model behind the scenes to develop the core business logic. The consumers were agnostic to what was happening behind the scenes, bringing in abstraction. This style also empowered developers and architects to deliver the business functionality by leveraging the choice of technology and programming language. The concept was simple—a piece of functionality was exposed through a web interface and accessible through a standard Internet protocol such as HTTP. This meant that any client could use the Internet to make RPC-like (Remote Procedure Call) calls to any server on the Internet and receive a response back as XML. The messages sent back and forth were encoded in a special XML dialect, called Simple Object Access Protocol (SOAP). The external clients could discover the web services using a discovery protocol called DISCO and then create a central repository of these services called Universal Description Discovery and Integration (UDDI).

Service Oriented Architecture

Next was the evolution to a service oriented architecture, which defined a way to make software components reusable and interoperable via a service interface. Services use a single common interface standard so they can quickly be incorporated and reused in new applications. This led to reuse and more composable patterns. This architecture pattern leveraged the web services design pattern while these web services could be exposed to the external world to consume a business functionality. Internally, that business functionality could be composed of multiple internal web services that worked together to deliver the business service. Each SOA service contained the code and data required to execute a complete, discrete business function (e.g., it could process a shopping cart, execute payment for the shopping trip, etc.).

This way, web services were then used to create a service oriented architecture. In order to connect an application to the data or functionality housed in another system, developers needed complex point-to-point integration—integration that developers had to recreate, in part or whole, for each new development project. Exposing those functions through SOA services allowed the developer to simply reuse the existing capability and connect through the SOA ESB architecture. Hence the enterprise service bus became the single point of orchestrating these services.

The architectural style of using the SOA provided many benefits. As the services evolved using SOAP, there came a new thought process, whereby the architecture needed services that were exchanging a lightweight payload as XML-based SOAP started getting heavy in scenarios in which a complex entity or messaged started getting exchanged. That is when Representational State Transfer Architectural (REST) was introduced so services could exchange messages and payload that was primarily based on JSON. These were very light as compared to SOAP. REST was designed specifically for working with components such as media components, files, or even objects on a hardware device. Any web service that is defined on the principles of REST can be called a RESTful web service. A RESTful service uses the normal HTTP verbs of GET, POST, PUT, and DELETE to work with the required components. In today's world, the RESTful web services are very popular.

Then came a new architectural style called *microservices,* which eventually became very popular. Everyone is talking about microservices because they seem like a solution to all of software's problems, such as new development, legacy modernization etc.

That takes you to the next topic—what are microservices and why do you need them? Are they the only solution, and all the rest should be thrown out? The next section address these questions.

What Are Microservices?

Microservices are nothing but a way of designing software applications as a set of services that are independent of each other; they can be deployed interpedently and follow their own independent lifecycle and versioning. No perfect definition can be found, but this architectural style is based on certain characteristics, based on how they are organized around business capability, called *domain-driven design*. Their deployment is automated end-to-end and follows the principles of intelligent endpoints and dumb pipes. This architectural style also provides decentralized control and governance and the freedom to use any programming language and any kind of database storage.

The pioneers in this field, James Lewis and Martin Fowler, have this to say about microservices:

> *The microservice architectural style is an approach to developing a single application as a suite of small services, each running in its own process and communicating with lightweight mechanisms, often an HTTP resource API. These services are built around business capabilities and independently deployable by fully automated deployment machinery. There is a bare minimum of centralized management of these services, which may be written in different programming languages and use different data storage technologies.*
>
> *—James Lewis and Martin Fowler (2014)*

The diagram in Figure 1-2 shows the microservices architecture.

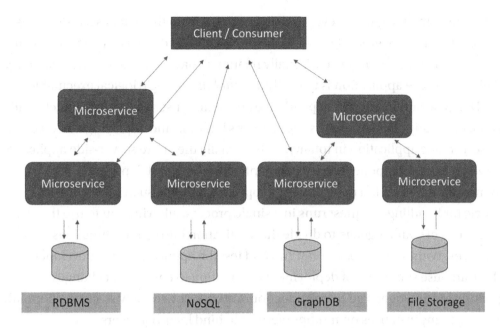

Figure 1-2. *Microservice architecture*

The question remains—why do you need the microservices architecture? Why can't you just leverage what you have in terms of services being called by various clients and external consumers? They can still consume the business functionality internally as well as externally when exposed over the Internet and you learned that web services using SOAP or RESTFul services already provide that leverage. So why microservices?

To better answer this question, you need to understand why, in some scenarios, the existing service-driven or service-oriented architecture is not good enough. It does not help enterprise grade customers, which are large enterprises that drive their business by leveraging software solutions.

Monoliths vs. Microservices

In order to appreciate and understand the microservice style, it's good to understand what problems exist with the architectural style of applications. A *monolith* application is built as a single unit, with all the components packaged in one single deployable unit. Enterprise applications are often built in three main parts: a client-side user interface (consisting of HTML pages and JavaScript running in a browser on the user's machine), and a server-side application. The server-side application handles the HTTP requests, executes the domain logic, retrieves and updates data from the database, and selects and populates HTML views to be sent to the browser and a database (consisting of many tables inserted into a common, and usually relational, database management system).

This server-side application is typically a *monolith*—a single logical executable or binary DLL or a combination of dependent executables or services. As the functionality gets enhanced, any changes to the system means building and deploying a new version of the server-side application in totality. So essentially the entire server-side application or its independent components have to completely rebuilt and deployed.

A monolithic server is a natural way to approach building such a system. All your logic for handling a request runs in a single process, allowing you to use the basic features of your language to divide the application into classes, functions, and namespaces. With some care, you can run and test the application on a developer's machine and use some type of deployment automation to ensure that changes are properly tested and deployed into production. You can horizontally scale the monolith by running many instances on multiple servers behind load-balancers.

Monolithic applications can be successful, but people are increasingly becoming frustrated with them—especially as more applications are being deployed at high frequencies. Enterprises bring in new ideas more frequently and they want to build and deploy those ideas into production quickly to get feedback from their customers. They cannot wait for months for a single service change to be deployed as a whole unit.

Change cycles are tied together—a change made to a small part of the application requires the entire monolith to be rebuilt and deployed. Over time, it's often hard to keep a good modular structure, making it harder to keep changes that ought to only affect one module within that module. Scaling requires scaling the entire application rather than parts of it.

The challenge was to determine how software changes could be deployed more frequently without having to deploy the entire software system and have the flexibility to deploy only the service that was enhanced without disturbing the remaining functionality. This led to the microservice architectural style, which is building applications as group of services. Services are independently deployable and scalable, and each service provides a firm module boundary, even allowing for different services to be written in different programming languages. They can also be managed by different teams.

A monolith application puts all its functionality into a single process, as depicted in Figure 1-3.

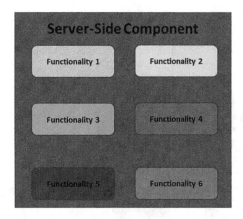

Figure 1-3. *A monolith server-side application*

The monolith scales by replicating itself on multiple servers, as depicted in Figure 1-4.

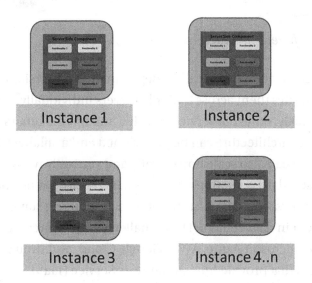

Figure 1-4. *Scaling a monolith*

The microservices architecture, on the other hand, puts each element of functionality into a separate service and has its own lifecycle and versioning that's independent of the other services. See Figure 1-5.

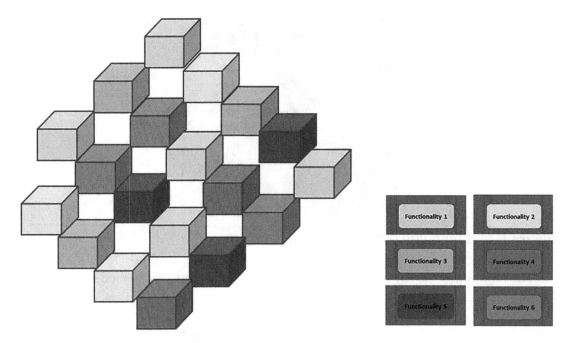

Figure 1-5. *Self-sufficient, isolated microservices*

The microservices style enables scaling, deployment, and versioning of services independently and scales them across multiple servers individually. If one service is being consumed quickly, only that service is scaled and not the others.

The microservices architecture can be provisioned and available for deployment on demand in no time . It can also scale horizontally and vertically when demand is high, and then shrink to standard operations when demand returns to normal.

These characteristics would be cost-prohibitive when using standard on-premise hardware deployment in data centers. These challenges are overcome by moving to cloud platforms like Microsoft Azure, AWS , Google Cloud, and similar cloud platform and service providers that provide Infrastructure as Service (IaaS), Platform as a Service (PaaS), and Software as a Service (SaaS) capabilities. This creates an ease at which microservices can be developed and deployed at scale and on demand, by leveraging modern methodologies. This is called *DevOps* (Development and Operations working as one team), and leads to a product development methodology rather than a project development methodology. This introduces the new area of cloud-native development The next section covers what cloud-native means.

Introduction to the Cloud-Native Architecture

Recall that monolith applications look somewhat like Figure 1-6. This is a typical business application that you can see in any enterprise.

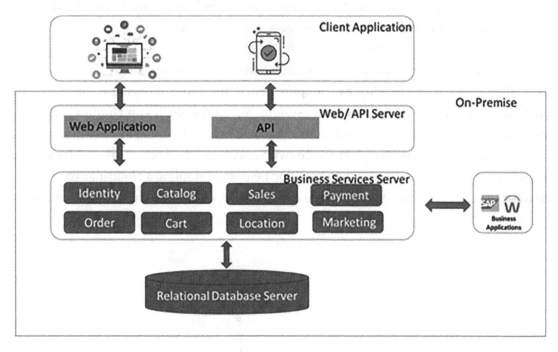

Figure 1-6. *Monolith business application*

You construct a large core application containing all of your domain logic. It includes modules such as identity, catalog, ordering, and more. The core app communicates with a large relational database. The core exposes functionality via an HTML interface.

Monoliths offer some distinct advantages. They are easy to

- Build

- Test

- Deploy

- Troubleshoot

- Scale

Many successful applications that exist today were created as monoliths. The app is a hit and continues to evolve, iteration after iteration, adding more functionality.

11

As the applications grows with more functionality, it becomes unmanageable. Developers find themselves losing control of the application. As time goes on, the feeling becomes more intense and they eventually enter a state where they are not sure of how the application will behave when a new functionality is introduced, as it has become unmanageable to govern and control. The application has become so overwhelmingly complicated that no single person understands it. Developers fear making changes because each change could have unintended and costly side effects. New features/ fixes become tricky, time-consuming, and expensive to implement. Each release is as small as possible and requires a full deployment of the entire application. One unstable component can crash the entire system. New technologies and frameworks aren't an option. It's difficult to implement agile delivery methodologies. Architectural erosion sets in as the codebase deteriorates with never-ending "special cases." Many organizations have addressed such monolithic beasts by adopting a cloud-native architecture. The application, when architected and deployed on a cloud, now looks like Figure 1-7.

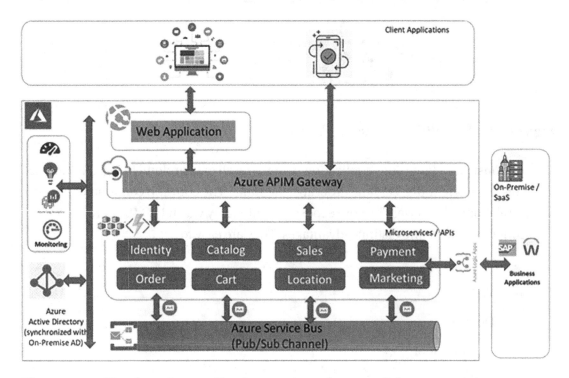

Figure 1-7. *Cloud-native application version of a monolith*

The application has been broken up across a set of small, isolated microservices. Each service is self-contained and encapsulates its own code, data, and dependencies. Each is deployed in a software container and managed by a container orchestrator. Instead of a large relational database, each service owns its datastore, the type of which vary based on the data needs. Note how some services depend on a relational database, but others on NoSQL databases. One service stores its state in a distributed cache. Note how all traffic is routed through an API gateway service that is responsible for directing traffic to the core backend services and enforcing many cross-cutting concerns. Most importantly, the application takes full advantage of the scalability, availability, and resiliency features found in modern cloud platforms.

So cloud-native is nothing but architecting applications using a modern architectural style like microservices and leveraging the cloud services that are natively available for building, testing, and deployment. It also leverages DevOps tooling like Azure DevOps.

Cloud-native is all about changing the way developers think about constructing critical business systems. It's designed to embrace rapid development and deployment. Frequent and faster changes, at a larger scale, build in resilience and high availability.

The Cloud-Native Computing Foundation (CNCF) defines cloud-native as follows:

> *Cloud-native technologies empower organizations to build and run scalable applications in modern, dynamic environments such as public, private, and hybrid clouds. Containers, service meshes, microservices, immutable infrastructure, and declarative APIs exemplify this approach.*

> *These techniques enable loosely coupled systems that are resilient, manageable, and observable. Combined with robust automation, they allow engineers to make high-impact changes frequently and predictably with minimal toil.*

Applications have become more and more complex, with users demanding more and more functionality. Business users expect rapid response and innovative features to be deployed with almost zero downtime. They expect minimum outages or no outages during maintenance and on-demand performance and scalability of applications. Cloud-native provides the speed and agility required to develop a line of business applications that are evolving from just being business capabilities to being more strategic transformations. They allow businesses to stay ahead of the game and continue to accelerate business growth.

Modern application development on cloud-native platforms is based on a widely accepted methodology called the *Twelve-Factor Application*. It describes a set of principles and practices that developers follow to construct applications optimized for modern cloud environments. Special attention is given to portability across environments.

While applicable to any web-based application, many practitioners consider Twelve-Factor a solid foundation for building cloud-native apps. Systems built on these principles can deploy and scale rapidly and add features to react quickly to market changes. The following points highlight the Twelve-Factor methodology:

- **Codebase**: A single codebase for each microservice, stored in its own repository. Tracked with version control, it can deploy to multiple environments (QA, staging, and production).

- **Dependencies**: Each microservice isolates and packages its own dependencies, embracing changes without impacting the entire system.

- **Configurations**: Configuration information is moved out of the microservice and externalized through a configuration management tool outside of the code. The same deployment can propagate across environments with the correct configuration applied.

- **Backing services**: Ancillary resources (datastores, caches, and message brokers) should be exposed via an addressable URL. Doing so decouples the resource from the application, enabling it to be interchangeable.

- **Build release run**: Each release must enforce a strict separation across the build, release, and run stages. Each should be tagged with a unique ID and support the ability to roll back. Modern CI/CD systems help fulfill this principle.

- **Processes**: Each microservice should execute in its own process, isolated from other running services. Externalize required state to a backing service such as a distributed cache or datastore.

- **Port binding**: Each microservice should be self-contained with its interfaces and functionality exposed on its own port. Doing so provides isolation from other microservices.

- **Concurrency**: Services scale out across a large number of small identical processes (copies) as opposed to scaling up a single large instance on the most powerful machine available.

- **Disposability**: Service instances should be disposable, favoring fast startups to increase scalability opportunities and graceful shutdowns to leave the system in a correct state. Docker containers, along with an orchestrator, inherently satisfy this requirement.

- **Dev/prod parity**: Keep environments across the application lifecycle as similar as possible, avoiding costly shortcuts. Here, the adoption of containers can greatly contribute by promoting the same execution environment.

- **Logging**: Treat logs generated by microservices as event streams. Process them with an event aggregator and propagate the data to data-mining/log management tools like Azure Monitor or Splunk and eventually long-term archival.

- **Admin processes**: Run administrative/management tasks as one-off processes. Tasks can include data cleanup and pulling analytics for a report. Tools executing these tasks should be invoked from the production environment, but separately from the application.

There are three other factors introduced for modern applications—API first design, telemetry, and Authentication and Authorization.

These applications need to also consider the following critical design considerations:

- **Communication**: How the frontend and backend communicate with each other and how microservices communicate with each other without introducing dependencies, possibly through loosely coupled messaging patterns like queues or a service bus.

- **Resiliency**: A microservices architecture moves your system from in-process to out-of-process network communication. In a distributed architecture, what happens when Service B isn't responding to a network call from Service A? Or, what happens when Service C becomes temporarily unavailable and other services calling it are blocked?

- **Distributed data**: By design, each microservice encapsulates its own data, exposing operations via its public interface. If so, how do you query data or implement a transaction across multiple services?

- **Identity**: How will your service identify who is accessing it and what permissions they have?

How Business Benefits from Cloud-Native Applications

In today's modern software development era, enterprises are driving business using technology and working toward digital transformation. Businesses need to be quick to introduce new ideas of innovation and deploy them before the competition.

Consider the following reasons that you would use a cloud-native application and microservices based architecture.

- Strategic enterprise system needs to constantly evolve business capabilities/features.

- An application requires a high release velocity, with high confidence.

- A system in which individual features must be released without a full redeployment of the entire system.

- An application developed by teams with expertise in different technology stacks.

- An application with components must scale independently and on demand.

- Nonfunctional requirements around performance of the existing application, scalability, and user experience should be baselined and accordingly.

- Dependencies on external and internal integrations need consideration to redesign the application and create a cloud-native architecture on a cloud platform.

- Monolithic apps are critical to the business and often benefit from a cloud-optimized lift-and-shift migration.

- Optimizations to deployments that enable key cloud services, without changing the core architecture of the application. As an example, you might containerize an application and deploy it to a container orchestrator, such as Azure Kubernetes Services, etc. Once in the cloud, the application can consume other cloud services such as databases, message queues, monitoring, and distributed caching.

- Finally, monolithic apps that perform strategic enterprise functions might best benefit from a cloud-native approach. This approach provides agility and velocity. But it comes at a cost of replatforming, rearchitecting, and rewriting code.

This cloud-native approach is appropriate if you focus on answering these questions—What exactly is the business problem that a cloud-native approach will solve? How would it align with business needs?

In scenarios in which the business drivers are not very demanding, a monolith can still serve business needs. The microservices architecture needs ease of deployment and on-demand scaling and availability, as well as application monitoring, logging, and telemetry. These nonfunctional requirements are provided by the cloud platforms but a more important quality is to scale on demand. That leads us to the world of containers and containerization. Microservices can be easily deployed on containers. But these containers need a mechanism to orchestrate, manage, and govern. That's where services like Kubernetes come into picture. Otherwise, the container management and orchestration will have to be developed and that is a complex area to develop at an enterprise scale. The next section introduces the Azure Kubernetes Service (AKS) and describes its components.

An Introduction to AKS and its Components

Now that you understand what microservices are and you know that cloud platforms provide native support to develop and deploy microservices, you can look at how containers can be utilized for deploying microservices. This section introduces Azure Kubernetes Service for this purpose.

Kubernetes is an open source orchestrator for deploying containerized applications. It was originally developed by Google, inspired by a decade of experience deploying scalable, reliable systems in containers via application-oriented APIs.

Since its introduction in 2014, Kubernetes has grown to be one of the largest and most popular open source projects in the world. It has become the standard API for building cloud-native applications, present in nearly every public cloud.

Kubernetes is a proven infrastructure for distributed systems and is suitable for cloud-native developers of all scales, from a cluster of Raspberry Pi computers to a warehouse full of the latest machines. It provides the software necessary to successfully build and deploy reliable, scalable distributed systems.

You may be wondering what is meant by "reliable, scalable distributed systems." More and more services can be delivered over the network via APIs. These APIs are often delivered by a distributed system, the various pieces that implement the API running on different machines, connected via the network and coordinating their actions via network communication. Because people rely on these APIs increasingly for all aspects of their daily lives (e.g., finding directions to the nearest hospital), these systems must be highly reliable. They cannot fail, even if a part of the system crashes or otherwise stops working. Likewise, they must maintain availability even during software rollouts or other maintenance events. Finally, because more of the world is online and using such services, they must be highly scalable so that they can grow their capacity and keep up with ever-increasing usage without radical redesign of the distributed system that implements the services.

There are many reasons that companies use containers and container APIs like Kubernetes, but they can all be traced back to one of the following benefits:

- Velocity

- Scaling (of both software and teams)

- Abstracting the infrastructure

- Efficiency

Containers are the base unit to be deployed in Azure Kubernetes Services.

Kubernetes is a platform for creating, deploying, and managing distributed applications.

These applications come in many different shapes and sizes, but ultimately, they are all comprised of one or more programs that run on individual machines.

These programs accept input, manipulate data, and then return the results. Before you can even consider building a distributed system, you must first consider how to build the application container images that contain these programs and make up the pieces of the distributed system.

Application programs are typically comprised of a language runtime, libraries, and the source code. In many cases, your application relies on external shared libraries. These external libraries are generally shipped as shared components in the OS that you have installed on a particular machine.

This dependency on shared libraries causes problems when an application developed on a programmer's machine has a dependency on a shared library that isn't available when the program is rolled out to the production OS. Even when the development and production environments share the same version of the OS, problems can occur when developers forget to include dependent asset files inside a package that they deploy to production.

The traditional methods of running multiple programs on a single machine require that all of these programs share the same versions of shared libraries on the system. If the different programs are developed by different teams or organizations, these shared dependencies add needless complexity and coupling between these teams.

A program can execute successfully only if it can be reliably deployed onto the machine where it should run. Too often the state of the art for deployment involves running imperative scripts, which inevitably have twisty and byzantine failure cases.

This makes the task of rolling out a new version of all or parts of a distributed system a difficult task.

When working with applications, it's often helpful to package them in a way that makes it easy to share them with others. Docker, the default container runtime engine, makes it easy to package an executable and push it to a remote registry where it can later be pulled by others. At the time of this writing, container registries are available in all of the major public clouds, and services to build images in the cloud are also available in many of them. You can also run your own registry using open source or commercial systems. These registries make it easy for users to manage and deploy private images, while image-builder services provide easy integration with continuous delivery systems.

Container images bundle a program and its dependencies into a single artifact under a root filesystem. The most popular container image format is the Docker image format, which has been standardized by the Open Container Initiative to the OCI image format. Kubernetes supports both Docker- and OCI-compatible images via Docker and other runtimes. Docker images also include additional metadata used by a container runtime to start a running application instance based on the contents of the container image.

Container Images

A container image is a binary package that encapsulates all of the files necessary to run a program inside of an OS container. Depending on how you first experiment with containers, you will either build a container image from your local filesystem or download a preexisting image from a container registry. In either case, once the container image is present on your computer, you can run that image to produce a running application inside an OS container.

The most popular and widespread container image format is the Docker image format, which was developed by the Docker open source project for packaging, distributing, and running containers using the docker command. Subsequently, work has begun by Docker, Inc. and others to standardize the container image format via the Open Container Initiative (OCI) project. While the OCI standard achieved a 1.0 release milestone in mid-2017, adoption of these standards is proceeding slowly. The Docker image format continues to be the de facto standard and is made up of a series of filesystem layers. Each layer adds, removes, or modifies files from the preceding layer in the filesystem. This is an example of an overlay filesystem. The overlay system is used both when packaging the image and when the image is being used.

During runtime, there are a variety of concrete implementations of such filesystems, including aufs, overlay, and overlay2.

The following sections look at the various components that drive the Kubernetes cluster.

The Cluster

At the highest level, Kubernetes is organized as a cluster of virtual or on-premises machines. These machines—called *nodes*—share compute, network, and storage resources. Each cluster has one master node connected to one or more worker nodes. The worker nodes are responsible for running groups of containerized applications and workloads, known as *pods,* and the master node manages which pods run on which worker nodes.

The Control Plane

In order for the master node to communicate with the worker nodes—and for a person to communicate with the master node—Kubernetes includes a number of objects that collectively form the control plane. Developers and operators interact with the cluster primarily through the master node by using kubectl, a command-line interface that installs on their local OS. Commands issued to the cluster through kubectl are received by the kube-apiserver, the Kubernetes API that resides on the master node. The kube-apiserver then communicates requests to the kube-controller-manager in the master node, which is in turn responsible for handling worker node operations. Commands from the master node are received by the kubelet on the worker nodes.

Deploying Apps and Workloads

The next step to getting started with Kubernetes is deploying apps and workloads. The master node maintains the current state of the Kubernetes cluster and configuration in the etcd, a key-value store database, at all times. To run pods with your containerized apps and workloads, you will describe a new desired state to the cluster in the form of a YAML file. The kube-controller-manager takes the YAML file and tasks the kube-scheduler with deciding which worker nodes the app or workload should run based on predetermined constraints. Working in concert with each worker node's kubelet, the kube-scheduler starts the pods, watches the state of the machines, and is overall responsible for the resource management.

Figure 1-8 shows how a typical Azure Kubernetes reference implementation would look.

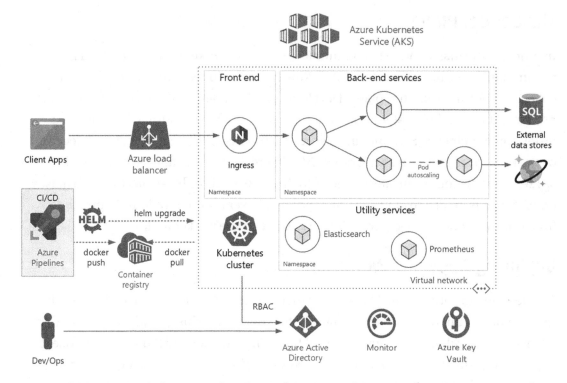

Figure 1-8. *Azure Kubernetes Service Reference Architecture (courtesy Microsoft Documentation for AKS)*

The components in Figure 1-8 are defined as follows:

- **Azure Kubernetes Service** is a managed Kubernetes cluster, hosted in the Azure Cloud Platform. When using AKS, Azure Manages the Kubernetes API service and you only need to manage the agent nodes.

- **Virtual Network** is needed to deploy the AKS cluster. By default, AKS creates a virtual network into which agent nodes are connected. More advanced scenarios can be handled by creating a custom virtual network before deploying the AKS cluster.

- **Ingress server** exposes HTTP(S) routes to services inside the cluster. You will learn about at this with more examples in subsequent chapters.

- **Azure load balancer** is created after creating the AKS cluster. The load balancer will be configured with a new public IP address that will frontend your ingress controller. This way the load balancer routes traffic to the ingress.

- **External datastores** are used to drive microservices data that comes from services like Azure SQL Database , Cosmos DB, and so on.

- **Azure Active Directory** is the key element to provide security to the cluster by creating an identity and managing other Azure resources. It is also used for Authentication and Authorization of users from client applications.

- **Azure Container Registry** stores private Docker images, which are deployed to the cluster. AKS can authenticate with Container Registry using its Azure AD identity. Note that AKS does not need Azure Container Registry. You can use other container registries, such as Docker Hub.

- **Helm** is a package manager for Kubernetes, which is a way to bundle and generalize Kubernetes objects into a single unit that can be published, deployed, versioned, and updated.

You saw how microservices benefit the business drivers and how cloud platforms like Microsoft Azure support the deployment of microservices. Azure Kubernetes Service is one of the ways to deploy microservices on the Azure platform.

Summary

This chapter described the evolution of the software development world and explained how the era of mainframes systems evolved to the client-server and service-oriented architectures.

You also learned about the various challenges of the architectural styles and how the microservices architecture was introduced, as well as the benefits it brings to the modern day business environment.

The chapter also covered cloud-native applications and how they benefit enterprise businesses. You looked at how businesses in today's era want to be ahead of competition and how cloud-native and microservices architecture helps them achieve this by making software development more rapid, scalable, and agile.

You were also introduced to containers and Azure Kubernetes Services and learned how microservices can leverage them to enable ease of deployment and scaling.

You have not seen any code in this chapter and that is on purpose, so that you can first understand why microservices are important and in what scenarios.

The next chapter includes an example to illustrate microservices and to explain important design considerations.

Appendix

https://martinfowler.com/microservices/

https://docs.microsoft.com/en-us/azure/architecture/reference-architectures/containers/aks-microservices/aks-microservices

https://www.cncf.io/

## CHAPTER 2

Microservices: Architecting and Design Considerations

Introduction

Now that you have learned about the evolution of distributed computing and have come to the modern-day patterns, which provide more robust, scalable, and quicker services, this chapter covers the microservice considerations of architecture and design.

You will then dive deep into what containers are and why you need frameworks and tools like Kubernetes.

Microservice Architecture Benefits

Why are organizations adopting microservices? What are the motivations and challenges? How can leaders of these organizations tell that taking on the challenges of managing a collection of small, loosely coupled, independently deployable services is paying off for the company? How do they measure success? The answers to these questions by the early adopters of microservices vary quite a bit. However, some common themes emerge and tie back to the mantra of "balancing speed and safety at scale."

Amazon describes the advantages of their architecture as follows:

We can scale our operation independently, maintain unparalleled system availability, and introduce new services quickly without the need for massive reconfiguration.

© Kasam Ahmed Shaikh and Shailesh S. Agaskar 2022
K. Ahmed Shaikh and S. S. Agaskar, *Azure Kubernetes Services with Microservices*,
https://doi.org/10.1007/978-1-4842-7809-3_2

By focusing on scalability and component independence, Amazon has been able to increase their speed of delivery while also improving the safety—in the form of scalability and availability—of their environment.

- Lessens dependencies between teams, resulting in faster code to production

- Allows lots of initiatives to run in parallel

- Supports multiple technologies/languages/frameworks

- Enables graceful degradation of service

- Promotes ease of innovation through disposable code—it is easy to fail and move on

The first three points help speed up software development, through organizational alignment and the ability to deploy independently, as well as polyglotism. The last two points speak to a safe environment that facilitates replaceability of services.

Social media pioneer Hootsuite has observed efficiency benefits in their microservice adoption based on the tunability of the system:

Some services require high availability, but are low volume, and it's the opposite for other services. A microservice approach allows us to tune for both situations, whereas in a monolith it's all or nothing.

The primary driver here is speed, as requested directly from the business. However, there is also an emphasis on safety—through ability to deploy independently and testability—as well as futureproofing through composability.

Embracing microservices, they were able to overcome this issue and improve the comprehensibility of their software system.

There are common goals and benefits that emerge from these implementation stories.

The goal of improving software delivery speed as functional scope grows is realized through greater agility, higher composability, improved comprehensibility, ability to deploy service independently, organizational alignment, and polyglotism. The goal of maintaining software system safety as scale increases is achieved through higher availability and resiliency, better efficiency, independent manageability and replaceability of components, increased runtime scalability, and more simplified testability.

Now that you understand these goals and benefits, let's explore how these goals and benefits derive business value for organizations that leverage microservice architecture.

Deriving Business Value

Successful companies focus on increasing software delivery speed, because they are compelled by the speed of their business. Similarly, the level of safety implemented in an organization's software system should be tied to specific business objectives. Conversely, the safety measures must not get in the way of the speed unnecessarily. Balance is required.

For each organization, that balance will be a function of its delivery speed, the safety of its systems, and the growth of the organization's functional scope and scale. Each organization will have its own balance. A media company that aims to reach the widest possible audience for its content may place a much higher value on delivery speed than a retail bank whose compliance requirements mandate specific measures around safety. Nonetheless, in an increasingly digital economy, more companies are recognizing that software development needs to become one of their core competencies.

In this new business environment, where disruptive competitors can cross industry boundaries or start up from scratch seemingly overnight, fast software delivery is essential to staying ahead of the competition and achieving sustainable growth. In fact, each of the microservice architecture benefits drive delivery speed and contribute real business value:

- *Agility* allows organizations to deliver new products, functions, and features more quickly and pivot more easily if needed.

- *Composability* reduces development time and provides a compound benefit through reusability over time.

- *Comprehensibility* of the software system simplifies development planning, increases accuracy, and allows new resources to come up to speed more quickly.

- *Independent deployability* of components gets new features into production more quickly and provides more flexible options for piloting and prototyping.

- *Organizational alignment* of services to teams reduces ramp-up time and encourages teams to build more complex products and features iteratively.

- *Polyglotism* permits the use of the right tools for the right task, thus accelerating technology introduction and increasing solution options. Likewise, digital native consumers expect always-on services and are not shy about changing corporate allegiances. Outages or lost information can cause them to take their business elsewhere. A safe software system is indispensable. The safety-aligned benefits discussed earlier also provide business value.

- Greater *efficiency* in the software system reduces infrastructure costs and reduces the risk of capacity-related service outages.

- *Independent manageability* contributes to improved efficiency and reduces the need for scheduled downtime.

- *Replaceability* of components reduces the technical debt that can lead to aging, unreliable environments.

- Stronger *resilience* and higher *availability* ensure a good customer experience.

- Better *runtime scalability* allows the software system to grow or shrink with the business.

- Improved *testability* allows the business to mitigate implementation risks. Clearly, microservice architecture has the potential to provide numerous business benefits. However, not every organization needs every benefit, and not every microservice architecture can deliver all of them.

Defining a Goal-Oriented, Layered Approach

Although microservice architecture was originally a reaction to the limitations of monolithic applications, there are many in the industry who think that new applications should still be built as monoliths first. The thinking is that only through the creation and ownership of a monolith can the right service boundaries be identified. This path is certainly well trodden, given that early microservice adopters generally went through the process of unbundling their own monolithic applications.

However, is a monolithic application architecture the only simple system starting point? Is it possible to start simple with a microservice? In fact, the complexity of a software system is driven by its scale. Scale comes in the form of functional scope, operational magnitude, and change frequency. The first companies to use microservice architecture made the switch from monolithic applications once they passed a certain scale threshold. With the benefit of hindsight, and with an analysis of the common goals and benefits of microservice architecture, you can map out a set of layered characteristics to consider when adopting microservice architecture.

Modularity

At its most basic level, microservice architecture is about breaking an application or system into smaller parts. A software system that is modularized arbitrarily will obviously have some limitations, but there is still a potential upside. Network accessible modularization facilitates automation and provides a concrete means of abstraction. Beyond that, some of the microservice architecture benefits discussed earlier already apply at this base layer.

To help software delivery speed, modularized services are independently deployable.

It is also possible to take a polyglot approach to tool and platform selection for individual services, regardless of what the service boundaries are. Also, the abstracted service interfaces allow for more granular testing.

This is the most technologically focused microservice architecture layer. In order to address this layer and achieve its associated benefits, you must establish a foundation for your microservice architecture.

Cohesiveness

Next to consider in your microservice architecture is the *cohesion* of services.

In order to have a cohesive microservice architecture, it must already be modularized. Achieving service cohesion comes from defining the right service boundaries and analyzing the semantics of the system. The concept of domains is useful at this layer, whether they are business-oriented or defined by some other axis.

A cohesive microservice architecture can enable software speed by aligning the system's services with the supporting organization's structure. It can also yield composable services that are permitted to change at the pace the business dictates, rather than through unnecessary dependencies. Reducing the dependencies of a system featuring cohesive services also facilitate replaceability of services. Moreover, service cohesion lessens the need for highly orchestrated message exchanges between components, thereby creating a more efficient system.

It takes a synthesized view of business, technology, and organizational considerations to build a cohesive system.

Interrelationships

The final and most advanced layer to consider in a microservice architecture is its system elements. After breaking the system into pieces through modularization, and addressing the services' contents through cohesion, it is time to examine the interrelationships between the services. This is where the greatest level of complexity in the system needs to be addressed, but also where the biggest and longest-lasting benefits can be realized.

Although a single service may be understandable even in a modularized microservice architecture, the overall software system is only comprehensible when the connectivity between services is known. Also, agility is only possible when the impacts of changes on the whole system can be identified and assessed rapidly. This applies on the safety side as well, where runtime scalability is concerned. Lastly, although individual components may be isolated and made resilient in a modularized or cohesive microservice architecture, the system availability is not assured unless the interdependencies of the components are understood.

Maturity Model for Microservice Architecture Goals and Benefits

These layered characteristics—modularized, cohesive, and inter-relationships identified—help to define a maturity model that serves several purposes. First, it classifies the benefits according to phase and goal (speed or safety), as discussed previously. Secondly, it illustrates the relative impact and priority of benefits as scale and complexity increase.

Lastly, it shows the activities needed to address each architectural phase. This maturity model is depicted Figure 2-1. Note that an organization's microservice architecture can be at different phases for different goals. Many companies have become systematized in their approach to safety—through automation and other operational considerations—without seeking the speed-aligned system-level benefits. The point of this model is not for every organization to achieve systematized actualization with their microservice architecture.

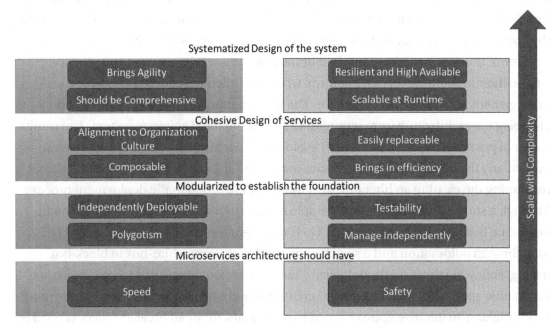

Figure 2-1. *A maturity model for microservice architecture goals and benefits*

Rather, the model is meant to clarify goals and benefits in order to help organizations focus their microservice strategies and prepare for what could come next.

Applying the Goal-Oriented, Layered Approach

Now you have a good understanding of how a microservice architecture can bring value to an organization, and a model for understanding what characteristics can bring what goals and benefits at what stage of adoption. But what about your organization? What are your business goals? What problems do you need to solve? It is a common misstep to start down the microservices path for its own sake without thinking about the specific benefits you are targeting. In other cases, some organizations aim for a high-level goal and then only implement one aspect of microservices while ignoring its founding conditions. For example, an organization with a high-level divide between development and operations—an organizational red flag—might execute a containerization strategy on their existing applications and then wonder why they didn't speed up their software development sufficiently. A broad perspective is needed.

To begin with, define the high-level business objectives you want to accomplish, and then weigh these against the dual goals of speed and safety. Within that context, consider the distinct benefits you are targeting. You can then use the maturity model to determine the complexity of the goal and identify the best approach to achieve it.

One of the digital media giants had initial attempts at microservice architecture was on their monolithic service platform, which included functions such as user management and license management. The first attempt was explicitly focused on changing the architecture from monolith to service-enabled software system. The results were not positive. However, when they evaluated the main issues with the application—particularly the operational inefficiencies around it—they changed their approach from refactoring the existing architecture to automating the problematic deployment process. Through a small investment, they were able to take their service platform deployment downtime from a week to 20 minutes. Their next iteration will focus on reducing QA time through automation and a switch in methodology from white-box to black-box testing. Following these methodological changes, they will identify the domains in their monolithic application that require the greatest speed of innovation and unbundle those first. By taking an iterative approach tied to clear goals, they can measure success quickly and change course if needed.

Microservices Design

So far you've learned that companies building applications in the microservices way do more than just implement small components. You now know that there isn't a strict definition for what constitutes a microservice architecture. Instead, the focus is on building applications that balance speed and safety at scale, primarily through replaceability.

But considering what you've learned about microservices systems so far, one thing should be clear—there are a lot of moving parts to consider. The hallmark of a microservice architecture might be smaller services, but following the microservices way will require you to think big. You'll need to tune your culture, organization, architecture, interfaces, and services in just the right way to gain the balance of speed and safety at scale.

The concepts introduced are rooted in some big domains: design, complexity, and systems thinking. But you don't need to be an expert in any of those fields to be a good microservice designer. Instead, the chapter highlights a model-driven way of thinking about your application that encapsulates the essential parts of complexity and systems thinking.

The Systems Approach to Microservices

Many first-time adopters of microservices tend to focus on the services that need to be built. But in order to develop applications in the microservices way, you'll need to conceptualize the design as much more than isolated, individual service designs. That doesn't mean that the design of services can be ignored—just like cars and pedestrians are essential to a traffic system, services are the key ingredient of a microservice system. But thinking in services terms alone isn't enough; instead you'll need to consider how all aspects of the system can work together to form an emergent behavior. Emergent behaviors are the ones that are greater than the sum of their parts and for a microservices application this includes the runtime behavior that emerges when you connect individual services together and the organizational behavior that gets you there.

A microservices system encompasses all the things about your organization that are related to the application it produces. This means that the structure of your organization, the people who work there, the way they work, and the outputs they produce are all important system factors. Equally important are runtime architectural elements such as service coordination, error handling, and operational practices. In addition to the wide breadth of subject matter that you need to consider, there is the additional challenge that all these elements are interconnected—a change to one part of the system can have an unforeseen impact on another part.

For example, changes to the size of an implementation team can have a profound impact on the work that the implementation team produces.

If you implement the right decisions at the right times, you can influence the behavior of the system and produce the behaviors you want. But that is often easier said than done. Grappling with all these system elements at the same time is difficult. In fact, you might find it especially challenging to conceptualize all the moving parts of the microservice system in your head.

Complexity scientists face a similar challenge when they work with complex systems.

With all the interconnected parts and the complex emergence that results, it is very difficult to understand how the parts work together. It is difficult to predict the results that can arise from a change to the system. So, they do what scientists have always done—they develop a model.

A model-based approach can help all of us conceptualize our system of study and will make it easier for us talk about the parts of the system.

With that in mind, Figure 2-2 depicts a microservice design model comprised of five parts: Service, Solution, Process and Tools, Organization, and Culture.

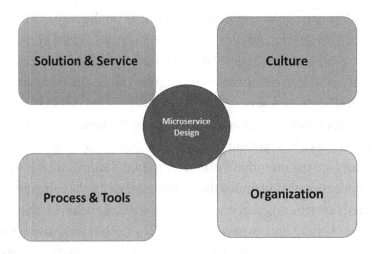

Figure 2-2. *The microservice system design model*

The goal of this model is to highlight the major areas of concern and the parts of the system you need to influence in order to succeed with this architectural style.

Service

Implementing well-designed microservices and APIs are essential to a microservice system. In a microservice system, the services form the atomic building blocks from which the entire organism is built. If you can get the design, scope, and granularity of your service just right, you'll be able to induce complex behavior from a set of components that are deceptively simple.

Solution

A solution architecture is distinct from the individual service design elements because it represents a macro view of the solution. When designing a particular microservice, your decisions are bounded by the need to produce a single output—the service itself. Conversely, when designing a solution architecture, your decisions are bounded by the need to coordinate all the inputs and outputs of multiple services.

This macro-level view of the system allows the designer to induce more desirable system behavior. For example, a solution architecture that provides discovery, safety, and routing features can reduce the complexity of individual services.

Process and Tools

Your microservice system is not just a byproduct of the service components that handle messages at runtime. The system behavior is also a result of the processes and tools that workers in the system use to do their job. In the microservice's system, this usually includes tooling and processes related to software development, code deployment, maintenance, and product management.

Choosing the right processes and tools is an important factor in producing good microservice system behavior. For example, adopting standardized processes like DevOps and Agile or tools like Docker containers can increase the changeability of your system.

Organization

How we work is often a product of who we work with and how we communicate.

From a microservice system perspective, organizational design includes the structure, direction of authority, granularity, and composition of teams. Many of the companies that have had success with microservice architecture point to their organizational design as a key ingredient. But organizational design is incredibly context-sensitive and you may find yourself in a terrible situation if you try to model your 1000+ employee enterprise structure after a 15-person startup (and vice versa).

A good microservice system designer understands the implications of changing these organizational properties and knows that good service design is a byproduct of good organizational design.

Culture

Of all the microservice system domains, culture is perhaps the most intangible yet may also be the most important. You can broadly define culture as a set of values, beliefs, or ideals that are shared by all the workers within an organization. Your organization's culture is important because it shapes all the atomic decisions that people within the system will make. This large scope of influence is what makes it such a powerful tool in your system design endeavor.

Much like organizational design, culture is a context-sensitive feature of your system.

What works in Japan may not work in the United States and what works in a large insurance firm may not work at an ecommerce company. So, you'll need to be cautious when attempting to emulate the practices that work in a company whose culture you admire. There is no recipe or playbook that will guarantee you the same results.

As important as it is, the culture of an organization is incredibly difficult to measure.

Formal methods of surveying and modeling exist, but many business and technology leaders evaluate the culture of their teams in a more instinctual way. You can get a sense of the culture of your organization through your daily interactions with team members, team products, and the customers they cater to.

Culture is often an indication of the impact of other parts of your system. Shared ideals shape how people do their work and how they work will in turn shape their organizational view. This is the interconnected nature of the system.

Embracing Change

Time is an essential element of a microservice system and failing to account for it is a grave mistake. All the decisions you make about the organization, culture, processes, services, and solutions should be rooted in the notion that change is inevitable.

You cannot afford to be purely deterministic in your system design; instead, you should design adaptability into the system as a feature.

There is good reason for taking this perspective: first, trying to determine what the end state of your organization and solution design should look like is a near impossible task. Second, it is unlikely that the context in which you made your design decisions will stay the same. Changes in requirements, markets, and technology all have a way of making today's good decisions obsolete very quickly.

A good microservice designer understands the need for adaptability and endeavors to continually improve the system instead of working to simply produce a solution.

Standardization and Coordination

Almost all of us work in organizations that operate within constraints. These constraints arise because the wrong type of system behavior can be harmful to the organization, even resulting in the organization failing as a result of particularly bad behavior. For example, a banking technology system that makes it easy to steal someone else's money or a tax system that fails to protect its users' private information are unacceptable.

With the cost of unwanted system behavior so high, it's no wonder that so many architects and designers do their best to control system behavior. In practice, the system designer decides that there is some behavior or expectation that must be universally applied to the actors within the system. Policies, governance, and audits are all introduced as a way of policing the behavior of the system and ensuring that the actors conform. In other words, some parts of the system are standardized.

But true control of this type of complex system is an illusion. You have as much chance of guaranteeing that your banking system will be perfectly secure as a farmer does of guaranteeing that his crops will always grow. No matter how many rules, checks, and governance methods you apply, you are always at the mercy of actors in a system that can make poor decisions.

Instead, all these mechanisms of control act as system influencers that greatly increase the likelihood of the results you want. Mastering the system you are designing and making it do the things you want requires you to develop the right standards, make sure the standards are being applied, and measure the results of the changes you are making.

However, control of the system comes at a steep price. Standardization is the enemy of adaptability and if you standardize too many parts of your system, you risk creating something that is costly and difficult to change.

Standardizing Process

You've read talked about how processes and tools are important for the behavior that emerges from your system. By standardizing the way that people work and the tools they use, you can influence the behavior in a more predictable way. For example, standardizing a deployment process that reduces the time for component deployment may improve the overall changeability of the system as the cost of new deployments decrease.

Standardizing how you work has broad-reaching implications on the type of work you can produce, the kind of people you hire, and the culture of your organization. The Agile methodology is a great example of process standardization. Agile institutionalizes the concept that change should be introduced in small measurable increments that allow the organization to handle change easier. One observable system impact for Agile teams are that the output they produce begins to change. Software releases become smaller and measurability becomes a feature of the product they output. There are usually follow-on effects to culture and organizational design.

In addition to process standardization, most companies employ some form of tool standardization as well. In fact, many large organizations have departments whose sole purpose is to define the types of tools their workers can utilize. For example, some firms forbid the use of open source software and limit their teams to the use of centrally approved software procured by a specialist team.

Standardizing Outputs

You can define a *team* as a group of workers who take a set of inputs and transform them into one or more outputs. Output standardization is way of setting a universal standard for what that output should look like. For example, in an assembly line the output of the line workers is standardized—everyone on the line must produce the same result. Any deviation from the standard output is considered a failure.

In a microservices system, a team takes a set of requirements and turns those into a microservice. So, the service is the output and the face of that output is the interface (or API) that provides access to the features and data the microservice provides. In fact, from the microservice consumer perspective, the API is the output, as they have no visibility of the implementation behind it.

In the microservices context, output standardization often means developing some standards for the APIs that expose the services. For example, you might decide that all the organization's services should have an HTTP interface or that all services should be capable of subscribing to and emitting events. Some organizations even standardize how the interfaces should be designed to improve the usability, changeability, and overall experience of using the service.

Standardizing People

You can also decide to standardize the types of people who do the work in your organization. For example, you could introduce a minimum skill requirement for anyone who wants to work on a microservice team. In fact, many of the companies that have shared microservice stories point to the skill level of their people as a primary characteristic of their success.

Standardizing skills or talent can be an effective way of introducing more autonomy into your microservices system. When the people who are implementing the services are more skilled they have a better chance of making decisions that will create the system behavior you want.

All organizations have some level of minimum skill and experience level for their workers, but organizations that prioritize skill standardization often set very high specialist requirements in order to reap system benefits. If only the best and brightest are good enough to work within your system, be prepared to pay a high cost to maintain that standard.

Standardization Trade-Offs

Standardizing helps you exert influence over your system, but you don't have to choose just one of these standards to utilize. But keep in mind that while they aren't mutually exclusive, the introduction of different modes of standardization can create unintended consequences in other parts of the system.

For example, you might decide to standardize on the APIs that all microservices expose because you want to reduce the cost of connecting things together in your solution architecture. To do this, you might prescribe a set of rules for the types of APIs that developers can create and institute a review process to police this standardization. As an example, many organizations standardize a way of documenting the interfaces that are created. Now Swagger (also called OpenAPI) is a popular example of an interface description language, but there are many others (WADL, Blueprint, RAML, etc.).

But you may find that constraining the types of APIs your people can produce limits the types of tools they can use to create them. It might be the case that the development tool you want everyone to use doesn't support the interface description language you have already chosen. In other words, the decision to standardize the team's output has had unintended consequences on the team's work process. This happens because standardization is an attempt to remove uncertainty from the system, but it comes at the cost of reducing innovation and changeability.

The benefit of standardization is a reduction in the set of all possible outcomes. It gives you a way to shape the system by setting constraints and boundaries for the actions that people within the system can take. But this benefit comes at a cost. Standardization also constrains the autonomy of individual decision-makers. The challenge for designers is to introduce just enough standardization to achieve the best emergent system outcome, while also employing standards and constraints that complement each other.

A Microservices Design Process

Professional designers know that the secret to great design is using the right design process. Where others apply expert advice or make false assumptions about the impact of their design decisions, a good designer employs a process that helps them continually get closer to the best product. This doesn't mean that you never have to make assumptions or that expert guidance is necessarily wrong. Instead, it means that your best chance at designing the microservice system you want is to work with a process that helps you understand the impact of your assumptions and the applicability of advice as you change the system. Figure 2-3 illustrates a framework for a design process that you can use in your own microservice system designs. In practice, it is likely that you'll need to customize the process to fit within your own unique constraints and context. You might end up using these design activities in a different order than given here. You may also decide that some activities aren't applicable to your goals or that other steps need to be added.

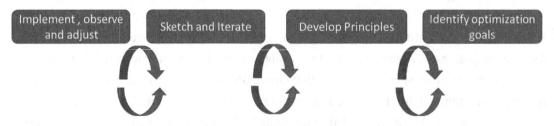

Figure 2-3. *Microservice system design process*

Set Optimization Goals

The behavior of your microservice system is "correct" when it helps you achieve your goals. There isn't a set of optimization goals that perfectly apply to all organizations, so one of your first tasks will be to identify the goals that make sense for your particular situation. The choice you make here is important—every decision in the design process after this is a trade-off made in favor of the optimization goal.

Note that optimization doesn't mean that other system qualities are undesirable. In fact, it is extremely likely that you will initially list many desirable outcomes for the system you create. But as you go through the system design process you will find that it is difficult to pull your system into many directions at the same time.

For example, a financial services information system might be optimized for reliability and security above all other factors. That doesn't mean that changeability, usability, and other system qualities are unimportant—it simply means that the designers will always make decisions that favor security and reliability above all other things.

It is possible that you may need to change your optimization goals at some point in the lifetime of your application. It just shows that you need to follow the design process and implement small changes to guide your system toward the new goal. If the goal change is quite different from your original design goal, this may take some time. If the optimization goal is radically different from your original goal, you may even create a new system design entirely.

Development Principles

Underpinning a system optimization goal is a set of principles. Principles outline the general policies, constraints, and ideals that should be applied universally to the actors within the system to guide decision-making and behavior. The best designed principles are simply stated, easy to understand, and have a profound impact on the system they act upon.

Sketch the System Design

If you find yourself building the application in a greenfield environment with no existing organization or solution architecture in place, it is important that you establish a good starting point for your system design. You won't be able to create the perfect system on your first try and you aren't likely to have the time or information to do that anyway. Instead, a good approach is to sketch the important parts of your system design for the purposes of evaluation and iteration.

How you do this is entirely up to you. There is a wealth of modeling and communication tools available to conceptualize organizational and solution architectures; choose the ones that work well for you. But the value of this step in the design process is to serialize some of the abstract concepts from your head into a tangible form that can be evaluated. The goal of a sketching exercise is to continually improve the design until you are comfortable moving forward.

The goal is to sketch out the core parts of your system, including organizational structure (how big are the teams? what is the direction of authority? who is on the team?), the solution architecture (how are services organized? what infrastructure must be in place?), the service design (what outputs? how big?), and the processes and tools (how do services get deployed? what tools are necessary?). You should evaluate these decisions against the goals and principles you've outlined earlier. Will your system foster those goals? Do the principles make sense? Do the principles need to change? Does the system design need to change? Sketching is powerful when the risk of starting over is small. Good sketches are easy to make and easy to destroy, so avoid modeling your system in a way that requires a heavy investment of time or effort. The more effort it takes to sketch your system the less likely you are to throw it away. At this early stage of system design, change should be cheap.

Most importantly, remember that the purpose of the iterative sketching stage is to participate in the process of designing. The goal is to form new ideas, consider the impact of proposed designs, and experiment in a safe way.

Implement, Observe, and Adjust

Bad designers make assumptions about how a system works, apply changes in the hope that it will produce desired behavior, and call it a day. Good designers make small system changes, assess the impact of those changes, and continually prod the system behavior toward a desired outcome. But a good design process is predicated on your ability to get feedback from the system you are designing. This is actually much more difficult than it sounds—the impact of a change to one small part of the system may result in a ripple of changes that impact other parts of your system with low visibility.

The perfect microservice system provides perfect information about all aspects of the system across all the domains of culture, organization, solution architecture, services, and process. Of course, this is unrealistic. It is more realistic to gain essential visibility into our system by identifying a few key measurements that give us the most valuable information about system behavior. In organizational design, this type of metric is known as a *key performance indicator* (KPI). The challenge for the microservice designer is to identify the right ones.

Gathering information about your system by identifying KPIs is useful, but being able to utilize those metrics to predict future behavior is incredibly valuable. One of the challenges that all system designers face is the uncertainty about the future. With perfect information about how the system might need to change, you could build boundaries in exactly the right places and make perfect decisions about the size of your services and teams.

Without perfect information, you are forced to make assumptions. Designers working on existing applications can observe the existing and past behavior of the system to identify patterns—components that change often, requirements that are always in flux, and services that can expect high usage. But designers who are working on new applications often have very little information to start with—the only way to identify the brittle points of the application is to ship the product and see what happens.

The risk of making poor decisions is that you steer the system in a direction that increases your "technical debt" (i.e., the future cost of addressing a technical deficiency). If you go too far along the wrong path, you risk producing a system that becomes too expensive to change, so you give up.

The classic microservices example of this is the cautionary tale of the "monolith." A team creates an initial release of an application when the feature set is small and the componentry has low complexity. Over time, the feature set grows and the complexity of the deployed application grows, making change ever more difficult. At this point, the team agrees that the application needs to be redesigned and modularized to improve its changeability. But the redesign work is continually deferred because the cost of that work is too high and difficult to justify.

At the other end of the scale is a system that is so overdesigned and overengineered for future flexibility that it becomes impractical. An incredibly complex, adaptable system that is built for massive amounts of change that never seems to happen.

Rather than trying to predict the future, a good microservices designer examines the current state and makes small, measurable changes to the system. This is a bit like taking a wrong turn on a long road trip—if you don't know that you've made a mistake you might not find out you're going the wrong way until it is too late to turn back.

A system that is designed with a high degree of visibility might give you a lot of information about what is happening, but if the cost of changing the system is too high you won't be able to make any course corrections. This problem of costly change presents itself when you need special permission, additional funds, more people, or more time to make the changes you want to the system.

So, in order to design a microservice system that is dynamic, you'll need to identify the right KPIs, be able to interpret the data, and make small, cheap changes to the system that can guide you back on the right course. This is possible only if the right organization, culture, processes, and system architecture are in place to make it cheap and easy to do so.

The Microservices System Designer

But you haven't identified who this system designer is or where they might fit into your existing organization.

To be most effective, the microservices system designer should be able to enact change to a wide array of system concerns. We've already identified that organization, culture, processes, solution architecture, and services are significant concerns for the system designer. But the boundaries of this system haven't been properly identified.

You could decide that the system boundaries should mirror the boundaries of the company. This means that the changes you enact could have a broad-reaching impact. Alternatively, you could focus on a department or service line within the company and build a system that aligns with the parent company's strategic goals. In fact, this type of nested set of systems is common and we see it all around us in the physical world (e.g., human beings and the entire human community).

Microservices system designer or as a matter of fact the software system designer is responsible for all the elements of the bounded system. The system designer's task is to introduce small changes within the system in order to produce behavior that will align with the desired goal. The solution architect focuses on the coordination of services, the team manager focuses on the people, and the service developer focuses on the service design. There should be a single person or a team who must be responsible for the holistic view of the entire system for a microservices system to succeed.

Goals and Principles

Regardless of the software architecture style you employ, it is important to have some overall goals and principles to help inform your design choices and guide the implementation efforts. This is especially true in companies where a higher degree of autonomy is provided to developer teams. The more autonomy you allow, the more guidance and context you need to provide to those teams.

This section looks at some general goals for a microservice architecture and some example principles. Along the way, we'll list our own suggested principles for you to consider.

Goals for the Microservices Way

It is a good idea to have a set of high-level goals to use as a guide when making decisions about what to do and how to go about doing it. We've already introduced the goal in building applications in the microservices way: finding the right harmony of speed and safety at scale. This overarching goal gives you a destination to aim for and given enough time, iterations, and persistence, will allow you to build a system that hits the right notes for your own organization.

There is of course a glaring problem with this strategy—it might take a very long time for you to find that perfect harmony of speed and safety at scale if you are starting from scratch. But thanks to the efforts of generations of technologists we have access to proven methods for boosting both speed and safety. So, you don't need to reinvent established software development practices. Instead, you can experiment with the parameters of those practices.

From our research, we've been able to distill four specific goals that lead to practices that aid both safety and speed of change. These goals aren't unique to microservice architecture, but they are useful in shaping your journey. Here are the four goals to consider:

- **Reduce costs**: Will this reduce overall cost of designing, implementing, and maintaining IT services?

- **Increase release speed**: Will this increase the speed at which your team can get from idea to deployment of services?

- **Improve resilience**: Will this improve the resilience of your service network?

- **Enable visibility**: Does this help you better see what is going on in your service network?

Let's look at these in a bit more depth.

Reduce Costs

The ability to reduce the cost of designing, implementing, and deploying services allows you more flexibility when deciding whether to create a service at all. For example, if the work of creating a new service component includes three months of design and review, six months of coding and testing, and two more weeks to get into production, that's a very high cost—one that you would likely think very carefully about before starting. However, if creating a new service component takes only a matter of a few weeks, you might be more likely to build the component and see if it can help solve an important problem. Reducing costs can increase your agility because it makes it more likely that you'll experiment with new ideas.

In the operations world, reducing costs was achieved by virtualizing hardware. By making the cost of a "server" almost trivial, it makes it more likely that you can spin up a bunch of servers in order to experiment with load testing, how a component will behave when interacting with others, and so on. For microservices, this means coming up with ways to reduce the cost of coding and connecting services together. Templated component stubs, standardized data-passing formats, and universal interfaces are all examples of reducing the costs of coding and connecting service components.

Increase Release Speed

Increasing the speed of the "from design to deploy" cycle is another common goal. A more useful way to view this goal is that you want to shorten the time between idea and deployment. Sometimes, you don't need to "go faster," you just need to take a shortcut. When you can get from idea to running example quickly, you have the chance to get feedback early, to learn from mistakes, and to iterate on the design more often before a final production release. Like the goal of reducing costs, the ability to increase speed can also lower the risk for attempting new product ideas or even things as simple as new, more efficient data-handling routines.

One place where you can increase speed is in the deployment process. By automating important elements of the deployment cycle, you can speed up the whole process of getting services into production. Some of the companies we talked with for this book spend a great deal of time building a highly effective deployment pipeline for their organization. Many of them have such a well-designed deployment model that they release to production multiple times a day. Automating release can go a long way toward increasing the speed of your microservice implementation and bringing in standardization and predictability.

Improve Resilience

No matter the speed or cost of solutions, it is also important to build systems that can "stand up" to unexpected failures. In other words, systems that don't crash, even when errors occur. When you have an overall system approach (not just focused on a single component or solution) you can aim for creating resilient systems. This goal is often much more reasonable than trying to create a single component that is totally free of bugs or errors. In fact, creating a component that will have zero bugs is often impossible and sometimes simply not worth the time and money it takes to try.

One of the ways DevOps practices has focused on improving resilience is through the use of automated testing. By making testing part of the build process, the tests are constantly run against checked-in code, which increases the chances of finding errors in the code. This covers the code, but not the errors that could occur at runtime.

There are companies that run what they call end-to-end tests before releasing to production but many companies rely on a practice that Jez Humble calls blue-green deployment. In this case, a new release is placed in production with a small subset of users and, if all goes well during a monitoring phase, more users are routed to the new release until the full userbase is on the new release. If any problems are encountered during this phased rollout, the users can all be returned to the previous release until problems are resolved and the process starts again.

Enable Visibility

Another key goal should be to enable runtime visibility. In other words, improve the ability of stakeholders to see and understand what is going on in the system. There is a good set of tools for enabling visibility during the coding process. You often get reports on the coding backlog, how many builds were created, the number of bugs in the system versus bug completed, and so on. But you also need visibility into the runtime system.

The DevOps practices of logging and monitoring are great examples of this level of runtime visibility. Most effort to date has been to log and monitor operation-level metrics (memory, storage, throughput, etc.). However, there are some monitoring tools that can act when things go badly (e.g., reroute traffic).

Trade-Offs

Each of these are important goals and sometimes they are competing goals. There are trade-offs to consider. You might be able to reduce your overall costs, but it might adversely affect runtime resilience. Or, you might be able to speed up deployment but that might mean you lose track of what services are running in production and reduce visibility into the larger service network. In the end, you'll need to balance various goals and find the right mix for your organization.

Your organization may have some other high-level goals you want to consider and document. Whatever these turn out to be, one of the next things you need to do is convert those goals into a set of actionable principles.

Operating Principles

Along with a set of goals for a microservice approach, it is important to have a set of principles. Unlike goals, which are general, principles offer more concrete guidance on how to act in order to achieve those goals. Principles are not rules—they don't set out required elements. Instead, they offer examples on how to act in identifiable situations.

Principles can also be used to inform best practices. Many of the organizations we looked at when doing research have their own set of principles within them company.

Netflix

One company that has been open about their own journey toward creating a successful microservice architecture is Netflix. We've called out just a few of Netflix's principles here.

Antifragility

Netflix works to strengthen their internal systems so that they can withstand unexpected problems. "The point of antifragility is that you always want a bit of stress in your system to make it stronger." There are several things Netflix does to promote this, including their "Simian Army" set of tools, which "enforce architectural principles, induce various kinds of failures, and test our ability to survive them". Software has bugs, operators make mistakes, and hardware fails. By creating failures in production under controlled conditions, developers are incentivized to learn to build more robust systems. Error reporting and recovery systems are regularly tested, and real failures are handled with minimal drama and customer impact.

Immutability

Immutability is used at Netflix to assert that auto-scaled groups of service instances are stateless and identical, which enables Netflix's system to "scale horizontally." The Chaos Monkey, a member of the Simian Army, removes instances regularly to enforce the immutable stateless service principle. Another related technique is the use of "Red/Black pushes". Although each released component is immutable, a new version of the service is introduced alongside the old version, on new instances, then traffic is redirected from old to new. After waiting to be sure all is well, the old instances are terminated.

Separation of Concerns

The Netflix microservice architecture arises because of separation of concerns (SoC) in the engineering team organization. Each team owns a group of services.

They own building, operating, and evolving those services, and present a stable agreed interface and service level agreement to the consumers of those services.

Invoking Conway's law, an organization structured with independent self-contained cells of engineers will naturally build what is now called a *microservice architecture*.

Three key principles: antifragility, immutability, and separation of concerns. Some of these same ideas were expressed slightly differently by Douglas McIlroy when describing the UNIX operating system.

UNIX

The following four points were offered as a set of "maxims that have gained currency among the builders and users of the UNIX system."

Here is the list that Douglas McIrloy and his colleagues called out:

1. Make each program do one thing well. To do a new job, build afresh rather than complicate old programs by adding new features.

2. Expect the output of every program to become the input to another, as yet unknown, program. Don't clutter output with extraneous information. Avoid stringently columnar or binary input formats. Don't insist on interactive input.

3. Design and build software, even operating systems, to be tried early, ideally within weeks. Don't hesitate to throw away the clumsy parts and rebuild them.

4. Use tools in preference to unskilled help to lighten a programming task, even if you must detour to build the tools and expect to throw some of them out after you've finished using them.

One of the interesting things about these four principles is that they offer general guidance on how to think about writing software. Phrases like "do one thing well" and "build software ... to be tried early" can lead developers to adopt what is known in the UNIX world as "The Rule of Parsimony" when writing code ("only write a big program when nothing else will do"). This, along with other UNIX rules, provides developers with a set of guidelines for which programming languages or libraries to use.

These principles are also meant to shape developers' thinking.

Suggested Principles

Having a set of principles to guide software developers and architects makes a lot of sense. There is no one set of principles that matches every company. Each organization needs to create a set that works for their company.

With this in mind, we offer a set of principles that reflect aspects of the other examples you've looked at so far. You can use these as starter material in putting together your own unique set for your company, or tune these until they fit.

Do One Thing Well

Many microservice implementations adopt the essential message—"do one thing well," which leads to the challenge of deciding what constitutes "one thing" in your implementation.

Build Afresh

The second part of McIlroy's first principle ("build afresh") is also important. Part of the UNIX philosophy is to create a collection of powerful tools that are predictable and consistent over a long period of time. It is worth considering this as an additional principle when implementing microservices. It may be better to build a new microservice component rather than attempt to take an existing component already in production and change it to do additional work. This also maps to Netflix's immutability principle.

Expect Output to Become Input

Another important principle for UNIX developers is the notion that one program's output is another program's input. For UNIX systems, this leads to reliance on text strings as the primary data-passing medium. On the Web, the data-passing medium is the media type (HTML, HAL, Siren, Collection+JSON, etc.). In some cases, you can even use HTTP's content-negotiation feature to allow API providers and consumers to decide for themselves at runtime which format will be used to pass data.

Don't Insist on Interactive Input

In the UNIX world, there is a desire to create scripts that tie a number of command-line tools together to create a "solution." This means humans don't need to be engaged every step of the way—the scripts handle both the input and the output on their own. Reducing the need for human interaction increases the likelihood that the component can be used in unexpected ways.

Human interaction isn't something that microservice components need to deal with at runtime. But when you expand your scope of focus to the microservice system, it's easy to find countless human interactions that could benefit from this principle. Reducing the dependency on human interaction in the software development process can go a long way toward increasing the speed at which change occurs.

Try Early

Adopting the point of view that your microservice components should be "tried early" fits well with the notion of continuous delivery and the desire to have speed as a goal for your implementations. Another advantage of this "try early" principle is you will learn your mistakes early. It turns out "try early" is also a way to encourage teams to get in the habit of releasing early and often. The earlier you release (even when that release is to a test environment), the earlier you get feedback and the quicker you can improve.

Don't Hesitate to Throw It Away

This is a difficult one for some developers. Being willing to throw something away can be hard when you've spent a great deal of time and effort building a component. However, when you adopt the "try early" principle, throwing away the early attempts is easier.

It is also important to consider this "throw it away" principle for components that have been running in production for a long time. Over time, components that did an important job may no longer be needed. You may have applied the "build afresh" principle and replaced this component with one that does the job better. It may be the case that the "one thing" that component does is simply no longer needed. The important thing is to be willing to throw away a component when it no longer serves its intended purpose.

Toolmaking

The "use tools" principle covers the notion that, when working to build a solution, you sometimes need to build the "right tool" for the job. One of the important elements in the developmental history of humans was the ability to create tools. These tools were created in order to reach a goal. In other words, tools are a means, not an end. This is also an important principle for microservice architecture.

While doing research for this book, we found several examples of companies that created their own developer and deployment tool chains in order to improve their overall developer experience. Sometimes these tools are built from existing open source software projects. Sometimes the tools are, themselves, passed into open source so that others can use them and contribute to improving and maintaining them. The important element here is to recognize that, in some cases, you may need to divert from building your solution and spend some time building tools to help you build that solution.

Platforms

Along with a set of general goals and concrete principles, you'll need tangible tools to make them real platform with which to make your microservice environment a reality. From a microservice architecture perspective, good platforms increase the harmonic balance between speed and safety of change at scale. We typically think about speed and safety as opposing properties that require a trade-off to be made but the right tooling and automation give you an opportunity to cheat the trade-off.

For example, the principle of immutability primarily improves the safety of changes that are made to the system. There is also an inherent release cost for immutability as each deployable unit needs its own associated release mechanisms, infrastructure, and management. On its own, the added cost can reduce the speed at which changes can be made. However, the introduction of containerization tools like Docker make independent deployment easy and greatly reduce the associated costs. When immutability is combined with containerization, both speed and safety of changes are optimized, which may explain the rapid adoption of Docker in large organizations.

The good news is that there are many examples of companies establishing—and even sharing—their microservice platforms. The challenge is that it seems every company is doing this their own way, which presents some choices to anyone who wants to build their own microservice environment. Do you just select one of the existing OSS platforms? Do you try to purchase one? Build one from scratch? It would be a mistake to just select one of the popular company's platforms and adopt it without careful consideration. Does this company provide the same types of services that mine does? Does this company optimize for the same things that mine will? Do we have similar staffing and training environments? Are our target customers similar (priorities, skills, desired outcomes, etc.)? Instead of focusing on a single existing company's platform, you should look at a general model for microservice platforms.

Shared Capabilities

It's common in large enterprises to create a shared set of services for everyone to use.

These are typically centered around the common infrastructure for the organization. For example, anything that deals with hardware (actual or virtual) falls into this category. Common database technologies (MySQL, Cassandra, etc.) and other software implemented infrastructure is another example of shared services.

These are standardized things like container technology, policy enforcement, service orchestration/interop, and data storage services. Even in large organizations it makes sense to narrow the choices for these elements in order to limit complexity and gain cost efficiencies. Essentially, these are all services that are provided to every team in the organization.

It is important to note that shared services does not mean shared instance or shared data. Just because all the teams use a single type of data storage technology (e.g., Mongo, Cassandra etc.) does not mean they all use the same running instance of the data storage and all read and write from the same tables.

While shared capabilities offer potential cost savings, they are ultimately rooted in the microservices goal of change safety. Organizations that highly value safety of changes are more likely to deploy centralized shared capabilities that can offer consistent, predictable results. On the other hand, organizations that desire speed at all costs are likely to avoid shared components as much as possible, as it has the potential to inhibit the speed at which decentralized change can be introduced. In these speed-centric companies, capability reuse is less important than speed of delivery. As with all things in the microservices way, you need to experiment with different forms of shared capabilities to see what works best for your unique context.

The following sections outline a high-level list of what shared services platforms usually provide.

Hardware Services

All organizations deal with the work of deploying OS- and protocol-level software infrastructure. In some companies there is a team of people who are charged with accepting shipments of hardware (e.g., 1-U servers), populating those machines with a baseline OS and common software for monitoring, health checks, and so on, and then placing that completed unit into a rack in the "server room" ready for use by application teams.

An alternate approach is to virtualize the OS and baseline software package as a virtual machine (VM). VMs make it possible to automate most of the work of populating a "new machine" and placing it into production.

A more recent trend is the use of containers to solve this problem. Docker is the most popular player in this field.

Source Code Management, Test, and Deployment

Once you have running servers as targets, you can deploy application code to them. That's where code management (e.g., source control and review), testing, and (eventually) deployment come in. There are quite a few options for all these services and some of them are tied to the developer environment, especially testing.

Most microservice shops go to considerable lengths to automate this part of the process. For example, the cloud platforms offers automation of testing and deployment that starts as soon a developer checks in their code. The process of automation can be involved and posting to production can be risky, so it is a good idea to treat this as a shared service that all teams learn to use.

Data Storage

There are many data storage platforms available today, from classic SQL-based systems to JSON document stores on through graph-style databases such as Neo4J.

It is usually not effective for large organizations to support all possible storage technologies. It makes sense for your organization to focus on a select few storage platforms and make those available to all your developer teams.

Service Orchestration

The technology behind service orchestration or service interoperability is another one that is commonly shared across all teams. There is a wide range of options here. Many of the flagship microservice companies wrote their own orchestration platforms.

Security and Identity

Platform-level security is another shared service. This often happens at the perimeter via gateways and proxies. Shared identity services are sometimes actually external to the company.

Architectural Policy

Finally, along with shared security, sometimes additional policy services are shared. These are services that are used to enforce company-specific patterns or models—often at runtime through a kind of inspection or even invasive testing.

One example of policy enforcement at runtime is Netflix's "Simian Army"—a set of services designed to purposely cause problems on the network (simulate missing packets, unresponsive services, etc.) to test the resiliency of the system.

Another kind of policy tooling is one that standardizes the way outages or other mishaps are handled after the fact. These kinds of after-action reviews are sometimes called postmortems. Whether in the form of runtime monitors or postmortem analysis, policy services ensure that varying teams adhere to the same guidance on how to handle both resiliency and security in their implementations.

Localized Capabilities

Localized capabilities are selected and maintained at the team or group level. One of the primary goals of the local capabilities set is to help teams become more self-sufficient. This allows them to work at their own pace and reduce the number of blocking factors a team will encounter while they work to accomplish their goals. Also, it is common to allow teams to make their own determination as to which developer tools, frameworks, support libraries, config utilities, and so on, are best for their assigned job. Sometimes these tools are selected from a curated set of "approved" products.

Most local capabilities services access and/or manipulate the shared service. Here's a list of the common local capabilities for microservice environments:

- **General tooling**—A key local capability is the power to automate the process of rolling out, monitoring, and managing VMs and deployment packages. Netflix created Asgard and Aminator for this. A popular open source tool for this is Jenkins and Azure DevOps.

- **Runtime configuration**—A pattern found in many organizations using microservices is the ability to roll out new features in a series of controlled stages. This allows teams to assess a new release's impact on the rest of the system (are we running slower, is there an unexpected bug in the release, etc.). Twitter's Decider configuration tool is used by a number of companies for this, including Pinterest, Gilt, and Twitter. Facebook created their own tool called Gatekeeper that does the same thing. Again, placing this power in the hands of the team that wrote and released the code is an important local capability.

- **Service discovery**—There are a handful of popular service discovery tools, including Apache Zookeeper, CoreOS' etcd, and HashiCorp's Consul. These tools make it possible to build and release services that, upon install, register themselves with a central source, and then allow other services to "discover" the exact address/location of each other at runtime. This ability to abstract the exact location of services allows various teams to make changes to the location of their own service deployments without fear of breaking some other team's existing running code.

- **Request routing**—Once you have machines and deployments up
  and running and discovering services, the actual process of handling
  requests begins. All systems use some kind of request-routing
  technology to convert external calls (usually over HTTP, WebSockets,
  etc.) into internal code execution (e.g., a function somewhere in
  the codebase). The simplest form of request routing is just exposing
  HTTP endpoints from a web server like Apache, Microsoft IIS,
  NodeJS, and others. However, as service requests scale up, it is
  common to "front" the web servers with specialized routing proxies
  or gateways. Netflix created Zuul to handle their routing.

There are popular open source services like Netty (created by JBoss) and Twitter's
Finagle.

- **System observability**—A big challenge in rapidly changing,
  distributed environments is getting a view of the running instances—
  seeing their failure/success rates, spotting bottlenecks in the
  system, and so on. There are quite a few tools for this. Twitter
  created (and open sourced) Zipkin for this task, and there are
  other similar frameworks that provide visibility into the state of the
  running system.

  There is another class of observability tooling—those that do more
  than report on system state. These tools actually take action when
  things seem to be going badly by rerouting traffic, alerting key
  team members, and so on. Netflix's Hystrix is one of those tools. It
  implements a pattern known as the Circuit Breaker to improve the
  resiliency of running systems.

Culture

Along with establishing goals and principles and arming your organization with the right
tools for managing platform, code, and runtime environments, there is another critical
foundation element to consider—your company culture. Culture is important because it
not only sets the tone for the way people behave inside an organization, but it also affects
the output of the group. The code your team produces is the result of the culture.

But what is culture? Quite a bit has been written about culture in general—from many perspectives including anthropological as well as organizational.

So, how does culture affect team output? And, if it does, what kinds of team culture improve team performance and work quality? We'll look at three aspects of culture that you should consider as a foundation for your microservice efforts:

- **Communication between teams:** Research shows that the way your teams communicate (both to each other and to other teams) has a direct measurable effect on the quality of your software.

- **Team alignment:** The size of your teams also influences output. More people on the team essentially means more overhead.

- **Fostering innovation:** Innovation can be disruptive to an organization, but it is essential to growth and long-term success.

Aligning Your Teams

Team alignment is important—it affects the quality of code. What can you do to take advantage of this information? Using the information from the start of this chapter, what "tunable" elements can you use to improve the alignment of your team structures to meet your goals for increasing speed, resilience, and visibility for your microservice efforts?

As the size of the group grows, the number of unique communication channels grows in a nonlinear way. This instance of combinatorial explosion is a common problem and needs to be kept in mind as you design your teams.

For example, Spotify, the Swedish music streaming company, relies on a team size of around seven (what they call a *squad*). They also rely on an aggregate of several teams that they call a *tribe* and reference There are several other factors in establishing your teams—including responsibilities, deliverables, and skillsets—that need to be present within a team.

Fostering Innovation

A third important element in managing company culture is fostering innovation within your organization. Many companies say they want to make innovative thinking common within the organization. And the ability to take advantage of creative and innovative ideas is sometimes cited as a reason to adopt a microservice approach to developing software. So it makes sense to spend a bit of time exploring what innovation looks like and how it can affect your organization.

A simple definition of innovate from Merriam-Webster's dictionary is "to do something in a new way; to have new ideas about how something can be done." It's worth noting that being innovative is most often focused on changing something that is already established. This is different than creating something new. Innovation is usually thought of as an opportunity to improve what a team or company already has or is currently doing.

A common challenge is that the innovation process can be very disruptive to an organization. Sometimes "changing the way we do things" is a needless or even threatening exercise—especially if the change will disrupt some part of the organization (e.g., result in eliminating tasks, reducing workload, or even replacing whole teams). For this reason, the act of innovating can be difficult. Another problem with innovation is that the process often looks chaotic from the outside. Innovating can mean coming up with ideas that might not work, that take time to get operating properly, or even start out as more costly and time consuming than the current practice.

Yet, many organizations really want to encourage innovative work within their teams.

Companies we talked to enable innovation by adopting a few key principles. First, they provide a level of autonomy to their teams. They allow teams to determine the best way to handle details within the team. Netflix calls this the principle of "context, not control." Team leaders are taught to provide context for the team's work and guidance on meeting goals, but to not control what the team does.

Second, companies that foster innovation build in a tolerance for some level of chaos. They operate with the understanding that it's okay if some things look a bit disorganized or messy. Of course, there are limits to this. Harvard Business Review's "Managing Innovation: Controlled Chaos" points out that "Effective managers of innovation ... administer primarily by setting goals, selecting key people, and establishing a few critical limits and decision points for intervention." Fostering innovation means setting boundaries that prevent teams from taking actions that threaten the health and welfare of the company and allowing teams to act on their own within these safe boundaries.

Managing communication channels, aligning teams, and establishing a safe place to innovate are all essential to enabling a successful culture that can take advantage of a microservice-style approach to designing, implementing, and maintaining software.

Summary

In this chapter, you learned the various design principles to derive at microservices. You also saw these various patterns being used.

You also learned how other companies likes AWS and Netflix have created strong patterns that you can leverage for your design and architecture for microservices.

The next chapter looks at microservices design patterns and shows how they are applied to an example application.

Appendix

https://netflixtechblog.com/the-netflix-simian-army-16e57fbab116

https://www.thoughtworks.com/insights/blog/demystifying-conways-law

https://homepage.cs.uri.edu/~thenry/resources/unix_art/ch01s06.html

https://www.atlassian.com/agile/agile-at-scale/spotify

## CHAPTER 3

Microservices Design Patterns

Introduction

Now that you have gone through the architectural and organizational considerations for assessing maturity and readiness for microservices, this chapter covers the design patterns that are used with microservices.

A sample example explains these design patterns and shows how they apply to microservices design.

Service Design

One of the key elements—the one most everyone thinks of when talking about microservice architecture—is the design of the actual microservice components themselves. It is these autonomous services that make up the fabric of the microservice system and do the actual work of implementing your solution strategy. Implementing systems that contain many small service components is a challenge so I devote an entire chapter to a set of tools and processes that can help you and your team take on the task.

In our experience working with various organizations and interviewing others, some of the more challenging questions that teams adopting microservice architecture face are how to properly size microservices ("how micro is micro?") and how to properly deal with data persistence in order to avoid sharing of data across services. These two concerns are actually closely related. A mistake in optimal sizing often begets the extraneous data-sharing problem, but the latter is especially problematic, operationally, since it can create tight cross-service coupling and impede independent deployability, a core value of the architectural style. Other topics that come up frequently when we talk

K. Ahmed Shaikh and S. S. Agaskar, *Azure Kubernetes Services with Microservices*,
https://doi.org/10.1007/978-1-4842-7809-3_3

with people who are designing and implementing microservices are things like support for asynchronous messaging, transaction modeling, and dealing with dependencies in a microservice environment. Getting a handle on these elements will help you curb the amount of additional (nonessential) complexity that creeps into your overall system. And doing that can help you in your constant struggle to balance the two key factors in any IT system: speed and safety.

This chapter covers microservice boundaries, looking at just how "micro" a service should be and why. It will explore microservice interfaces (APIs), discussing the importance of evolvable, message-oriented APIs for microservices and how they can reduce intercomponent coupling. It will investigate effective data storage approaches for microservices, exploring the power of shifting from data-centric and state-capturing models toward capability-driven and event-sourcing-oriented ones.

The chapter also shows how the command query responsibility segregation (CQRS) pattern can improve the granularity of data services, while maintaining sufficient speed and safety.

By the time you get through this material, you should have a good understanding of the challenges as well as the available patterns and practices you can use when it comes to designing and building microservice components.

Let's get started with the big one: "What is the optimal size of a microservice?"

Microservice Boundaries

So just how *micro* should a microservice be? There is no simple answer to this question. The things that first come to mind, such as lines of code in a microservice or the size of a team working on one, are compelling, since they offer the chance to focus on a quantifiable value (e.g., "The answer is 40"). However, the problem with these measures is that they ignore the business context of what you are implementing. They don't address the organizational context of who is implementing the service and, more importantly, how the service is being used within your system.

Instead of trying to find some quantity to measure, most companies focus on a quality of each microservice—the use case or context in which the component will be used. Many microservice adopters have turned to Eric Evans' "domain-driven design" (DDD) approach for a well-established set of processes and practices that facilitate effective, business-context–friendly modularization of large complex systems.

Microservice Boundaries and Domain-Driven Design

Essentially, what we see people doing when they introduce the microservices way into their companies is that they begin to decompose existing components into smaller parts in order to increase their ability to improve the quality of the service faster without sacrificing reliability.

There are many ways to decompose a large system into smaller subsystems. In one case you may be tempted to decompose a system based on implementation technology.

For instance, you can say that all computationally heavy services need to be written in C or Rust or Go (choose your own poison) and therefore they are a separate subsystem, while I/O-heavy features could certainly benefit from the nonblocking I/O of a technology such as Node.js and therefore they are a subsystem of their own. Alternatively, you can divide a large system based on team geography: one subsystem may be written in the United States, while others may be developed and maintained by software teams in Africa, Asia, Australia, Europe, or South America. Intuitively, giving a self-contained subsystem for development to a team that is in one place is well optimized.

Another reason you may decide to divide a system based on geography is that specific legal, commercial, and cultural requirements of operating in a particular market may be better understood by a local team. Can a software development team from New York accurately capture all the necessary details of an accounting software that will be used in Cairo?

A fresh approach to determining boundaries of subsystems in the context of a larger system. The process, offers a model-centric view of software system design. As pointed out, models are a great way to view a system. They provide an abstract way to look at something—a way that highlights the things you are interested in. Models are a point of view.

It's Only a Model

To understand the DDD approach, it is important to remember that any software system is a model of a reality—it is not the reality itself. For instance, when you log in to online banking and are looking at your checking account, you are not looking at the actual checking account. You're just looking at a representation—a model—that gives you information about the checking account such as balance and past transactions. It's likely that the screen your bank teller sees when looking at your account has different information because it's another model of your account.

Most large systems don't actually have a single model. The overall model of a large system is comprised of many smaller models that are intermingled. These smaller models are organic representations of relevant business contexts—they make sense in their context and when used within the context they are intuitive for a person who is the subject matter expert of the context.

Bounded Context

When working with models, teams need to be very careful when combining contextual models to form a larger software system. Multiple models are in play on any large project. Yet when code based on distinct models is combined, software becomes buggy, unreliable, and difficult to understand. Communication among team members becomes confused. It is often unclear in what context a model should not be applied. This concept was thought of well before microservices term was coined.

Yet, the preceding quotation is an important observation about the nature of modeling—if you try to rely on a single model (e.g., a canonical model) things become difficult to understand. The microservices way attempts to break large components (models) into smaller ones in order to reduce the confusion and bring more clarity to each element of the system. As such, microservice architecture is an architectural style that is highly compatible with the DDD way of modeling. To aid in this process of creating smaller, more coherent components, the bounded contexts concept was introduced. Each component in the system lives within its own bounded context, which means the model for each component and these context models are only used within their bounded scope and are not shared across the bounded contexts.

It is generally acknowledged that properly identifying bounded contexts in a system, using DDD techniques, and breaking up a large system along the seams of those bounded contexts is an effective way of designing microservice boundaries. If you use the DDD and bounded contexts approaches, the chances of two microservices needing to share a model and the corresponding data space, or ending up having tight coupling, are much lower. Avoiding data sharing improves the ability to treat each microservice as an independently deployable unit.

Using DDD and bounded contexts is an excellent process for designing components. However, there is more to the story. You could actually use DDD and still end up creating fairly large components. But large is not what you're going for in a microservice architecture. Instead, you're aiming at small—micro, even. And that leads to an important aspect of designing microservice components—smaller is better.

Smaller Is Better

The notion of work-unit granularity is a crucial one in many contexts of modern software development. Whether defined explicitly or implicitly, you can clearly see the trend showing up in such foundational methodologies as Agile Development, Lean Startup, and Continuous Delivery, among others. These methodologies have revolutionized project management, product development, and DevOps, respectively.

It is interesting to note that each one of them has the principle of size reduction at its core: reducing the size or scope of the problem, reducing the time it takes to complete a task, reducing the time it takes to get feedback, and reducing the size of the deployment unit. These all fall into a notion we call "batch-size reduction."

For example, here's an excerpt from the Agile Manifesto:

Deliver working software frequently, from a couple of weeks to a couple of months, with a preference to the shorter timescale.

—The Agile Manifesto, Kent Beck et al.

Basically, moving to Agile from Waterfall can be viewed as a reduction of the "batch size" of a development cycle—if the cycle was taking many months in Waterfall, now you strive to complete a similar batch of tasks: define, architect, design, develop, and deploy, in much shorter cycles (weeks versus months). Granted, the Agile Manifesto lists other important principles as well, but they only reinforce and complement the core principle of "shorter cycles" (i.e., reduced batch size).

The principal benefits of Continuous Delivery, Martin Fowler is unambiguous about the role of small batch sizes, calling it the precondition for a core benefit of the methodology.

Once you adopt the notion of limited batch size from Agile, Lean, and Continuous Delivery at the code, project, and deployment level, it makes sense to think about applying it at the architecture level as well. And many of the companies we interviewed have done this. After all, architecture is the direct counterpart to the other three disciplines. So, in the simplest terms, this "limited batch size" is the "micro" in microservice.

Just as in Agile, etc., there's no simple, universal measure for determining just "how small" a microservice should be (e.g., a quantity).

What people tell us is that they use the word "small" as a quality like "reliable" and "coherent," etc.

Ubiquitous Language

Just by stating a simple preference of "smaller is better," you'll immediately run into a problem if bounded contexts are your only tool for sizing microservices, because bounded contexts cannot actually be arbitrarily small. Here's what one of the prominent authorities in the space of DDD, Vaughn Vernon, had to say about the optimal size of a bounded context:

In DDD, we need a shared understanding and way of expressing the domain specifics. This shared understanding should provide business and tech teams with a common language that they can use to collaborate on the definition and implementation of a model. Just as DDD tells us to use one model within a component (the bounded context), the language used within that bounded context should be coherent and pervasive—what we in DDD call ubiquitous language.

From a purely technical perspective, the smaller the microservice the easier it can be developed quicker (Agile), iterated on quicker (Lean), and deployed more frequently (Continuous Delivery). But on the modeling side, it is important to avoid creating services that are "too small." According to Vernon, we cannot arbitrarily reduce the size of a bounded context because its optimal size is determined by the business context (model). The technical need for the size of a service can sometimes be different (smaller) from what DDD modeling can facilitate. This is probably why Sam Newman, very carefully, called bounded context analysis an "excellent start," but not the sole prescription for how to size microservices. And we completely agree. Bounded contexts are a great start, but you need more tools in your toolbelt if you are to size microservices efficiently.

API Design for Microservices

When considering microservice component boundaries, the source code itself is only part of the concern. Microservice components only become valuable when they can communicate with other components in the system. They each have an interface or API. Just as you need to achieve a high level of separation, independence, and modularity of the code, you need to make sure that your APIs, the component interfaces, are also loosely coupled. Otherwise, you can't deploy two microservices independently, which is one of the primary goals in order to balance speed and safety.

There are two practices in crafting APIs for microservices worth mentioning here:

- Message-oriented
- Hypermedia-driven

Message-Oriented

Just as you work to write component code that can be safely refactored over time, you need to apply the same efforts to the shared interfaces between components. The most effective way to do this is to adopt a message-oriented implementation for microservice APIs. The notion of messaging as a way to share information between components dates back to the initial ideas about how object-oriented programming would work.

All of the companies we talked with about microservice component design mentioned the notion of messaging as a key design practice. For example, Netflix relies on message formats like Avro, Protobuf, and Thrift over TCP/IP for communicating internally and JSON over HTTP for communicating to external consumers (e.g., mobile phones, browsers, etc.). By adopting a message-oriented approach, developers can expose general entry points into a component (e.g., an IP address and port number) and receive task-specific messages at the same time. This allows changes in message content as a way of refactoring components safely over time. The key lesson learned here is that for far too long, developers have viewed APIs and web services as tools to transmit serialized "objects" over the wire. However, a more efficient approach is to look at a complex system as a collection of services exchanging messages over a wire.

Hypermedia-Driven

Some companies we spoke to are taking the notion of message-oriented to the next level. They are relying on hypermedia-driven implementations. In these instances, the messages passed between components contain more than just data. The messages also contain descriptions of possible actions (e.g., links and forms). Now, not just the data is loosely coupled—so are the actions. For example, Amazon's API Gateway and App- Stream APIs both support responses in the Hypertext Application Language (HAL) format.

Hypermedia-style APIs embrace evolvability and loose coupling as the core values of the design style. You may also know this style as APIs with Hypermedia As The Engine Of Application State (HATEOAS APIs). Regardless of the name used, if you are to design proper APIs in microservice architecture, it helps to get familiar with the hypermedia style.

Hypermedia style is essentially how HTML works for the browser. HTTP messages are sent to an IP address (your server or client location on the Internet) and a port number (usually "80" or "443"). The messages contain the data and actions encoded in HTML format. For example, a message that contains information on an outstanding shipment due to arrive at your office might look like this:

```
<html>
<head>
<title>Shipment #123</title>
</head>
<body>
<h1>Shipment #123</h1>
<div id="data">
<span>ID: 123</span><br />
<span>Description: Widget Covers</span><br />
<span>Quantity: 1 Gross</span><br />
<span>Estimated Arrival: 2017-01-09</span><br />
</div>
<div id="actions">
<a href="...">Refresh</a>
<a href="...">Exit</a>
<form method="get" action="...">
<input name="id" value="" />
<input type="submit" value="Search" />
</form>
</div>
</html>
```

The hypermedia API style is as transformative to the API space as object-oriented design was for code design. A long time ago, we used to just write endless lines of code (maybe lightly organizing them in functions), but then object-oriented design came by with a revolutionary idea: "what if we grouped the state and the methods that operate on that state in an autonomous unit called an object, thus encapsulating data and behavior?" In essence, hypermedia style has very similar approach but for API design. This is an API style in which API messages contain both data and controls (e.g., metadata, links, forms), thus dynamically guiding API clients by responding with not just static data but also control metadata describing API affordances (i.e., "what can I do with this API?").

Exposing affordances makes sense for services that communicate over the Web. If you look at the Web as both the human-centric Web (websites consumed by humans) and machine Web (APIs), you can see stark differences in how far behind the machine Web is. When you load a web page on the human-centric Web, it doesn't just give you content (text, photos, videos, etc.)—most web pages also contain links to related content or search menus: something you can interact with. Basically, web pages tell you, in the response itself, what else you can do. Conventional Web APIs don't do this.

Most contemporary RESTful (CRUD) APIs respond with just data and then you have to go and read some documentation to find out what else can be done. Most people would agree that it would be quite a ridiculous experience. The human Web wouldn't be very functional if the responses didn't contain behavioral affordances. But that's exactly the case for most modern RESTful APIs. And, as a matter of fact, the data only approach is quite as brittle and dysfunctional for the machine Web as the picture painted for the human-centric Web, except we have gotten used to the unfortunate state of affairs.

Hypermedia APIs are more like the human Web: evolvable, adaptable, versioning free—when was the last time you cared about what "version" of a website you are looking at? As such, hypermedia-style APIs are less brittle, more discoverable, and fit right at home in a highly distributed, collaborative architectural style such as microservices.

Data and Microservices

As software engineers, we have been trained to think in terms of data, first and foremost.

To give the simplest example, it has pretty much been ingrained in our "muscle memory," or whatever the mental equivalent of one is, to start system design by first designing the pertinent data models. When asked to build an application, the very first task most software engineers will complete is identifying entities and designing database tables for data storage. This is an efficient way of designing centralized systems and whole generations of programmers have been trained to think this way. But data-centric design is not a good way to implement distributed systems—especially systems that rely on independently deployable microservices. The biggest reason for this is the absence of strong, centralized, uniform control over the entire system in the case of distributed systems, which makes a formerly efficient process inefficient.

The first step in breaking the data-centric habit is to rethink our system designs. It turns out that capabilities-centric design is more suitable for microservices than a more traditional, data-centric design.

Shipping Company Example

Assume that you are designing a microservice architecture for a fledgling shipment company, aptly named Shipping Company. As a parcel-delivery company, they need to accept packages, route them through various sorting warehouses (hops on the route), and eventually deliver to the destination. Because it is 2021 and the company is very tech-savvy, Shipping Company is building native mobile applications for a variety of platforms to let customers track their packages all the way from pickup to final delivery. These mobile applications will get the data and functionality they need from a set of microservices.

Let's imagine that Shipping Company's accounting and sales subsystems (microservices) need access to daily currency exchange rates to perform their operations. A datacentric design would create a table or set of tables in a database that contain exchange rates. Then we would let various subsystems query our database to retrieve the data.

This solution has significant issues—two microservices depend on the design of the shared table and data in it, leading to tight coupling and impeding independent deployment.

If instead, we had viewed "currency exchange rates" as a capability and had built an independent microservice (currency rates) serving the sales and accounting microservices, we would have had three independent services, all loosely coupled and independently deployable. Furthermore, since, by their nature, APIs in services hide implementation details, we can completely change the data persistence supporting the currency rates service (e.g., from MySQL to Cassandra, if scalability became an issue) without any of the service's consumers noticing the change or needing to adjust. Last but not least, since services (APIs) are able to put forward alternative interfaces to its various consumers, we can easily alter the interface that the currency rates microservice provides to the sales microservice, without affecting the accounting microservice, thus fulfilling the promise of independent evolution, a necessity for independent deployment.

Thinking in terms of capabilities rather than data is a very powerful technique for API design, in general. It usually results in a more use-case-oriented interface (instead of an SQL-like data-object interface). A capabilities-centric API design is usually a good approach, but in the case of microservices it is not just a smart design technique, it's a powerful way of avoiding tight coupling. You just saw evidence of this.

Much like bounded context analysis, capabilities-oriented design is a crucial technique but not enough to ensure independent deployment for all use cases. Not every example is as simple as the currency rates one. You cannot always encapsulate shared data inside a microservice and call it a day. For example, a common use case that cannot be solved with encapsulated capabilities is that of reporting. Any business application requires a certain level of reporting. And reporting often spans across multiple models, bounded contexts, and capabilities. Should reporting-oriented microservices be allowed to share tables with other microservices? The obvious answer is no, because that would immediately create severe tight coupling of services all around the system, and at the very least undermine (if not completely kill) independent deployment.

Let's see what techniques you can use to avoid data-sharing in complex use cases. The first one is event sourcing, a powerful data-modeling methodology that can help you avoid data-sharing in microservices, even in very complicated cases. The second, related methodology is CQRS—command query responsibility segregation.

Event Sourcing

Recall that there are some deeply ingrained software engineering habits that greatly affect the way people typically approach systems engineering. One of the most widespread of those habits is structural data modeling. It has become very natural for developers to describe models as collections of interacting logical entities and then to map those logical entities to physical tables where the data is stored. More recently, people have started using NoSQL and object stores that take them slightly away from the relational world, but in essence the approach is still the same: you design structural entities that model objects around you and then "save" the object's state in a database store of some kind. Whether storage happens in table rows and columns, serialized as JSON strings, or as object graphs, you are still performing CRUD-based modeling.

But this is not the only way to model the world. Instead of storing structures that model the state of the world, you can store events that lead to the current state of the world. This modeling approach is called event sourcing.

It is fair to note that for most software developers used to structural data modeling, event sourcing will initially sound alien and, maybe, even somewhat weird.

But it really isn't. For one thing, event sourcing is not some bleeding-edge, untested theory dreamed up to solve problems in microservices. Event sourcing has been used in the financial industry with great success, independent of any microservice architecture association.

In addition, the roots and inspiration for event sourcing go way beyond microservices, the Internet itself, or even computers—all the way back to financial accounting and the paper-and-pen ledgers that contain a list of transactions, and never just the end value ("state") of a balance. Think of your bank account: there's a balance amount for your checking and savings accounts, but those are not first-class values that banks store in their databases. The account balance is always a derivative value; it's a function.

More specifically, the balance is the sum of all transactions from the day you opened your account.

To dispute your current balance, your bank won't go to the error, which is very system specific and raw. Instead, they will print out all relevant transactions for you (or point you to online banking where you can do it yourself) and let you verify that the result of the transactions should indeed equal the balance value displayed. If you do find an error with any of the transactions, the bank will issue a "compensating transaction" to fix the error. This is another crucial property of event sourcing: much like in life, we can never go back in time and change the past. We can only do something in the present to compensate for the mistakes of the past. In event sourcing, data is immutable—we always issue a new command/event to compensate rather than update a state of an entity, as we would do in a CRUD style.

When event sourcing is introduced to developers, the immediate concern is usually performance. If any state value is a function of events, we may assume that every access to the value would require recalculation of the current state from the source events. Obviously that would be extremely slow and generally unacceptable. Fortunately, in event sourcing, we can avoid such expensive operations by using a so-called rolling snapshot—a projection of the entity state at a given point in time. Depending on the event source implementation, it is common to snapshot intermediary values at various time points. For instance, you may precalculated your bank account balance on the last day of every month, so that if you need the balance on January 15, 2021 you will already have it on December 31, 2020 and will just need to calculate the projection for two weeks, instead of the entire life of the bank account. The specifics of how you implement rolling snapshots and projections may depend on the context of your application.

Despite its accounting roots, event sourcing is not only relevant to just financial use cases. The rest of this chapter uses a business scenario as far from banking and accounting as you could imagine—shipment and delivery of goods.

As a parcel-delivery company, Shipping Company needs to accept packages, route them through various sorting warehouses (hops on the route), and eventually deliver them to their destinations.

A representative data model for this system executed in structural style is shown in Figure 3-1.

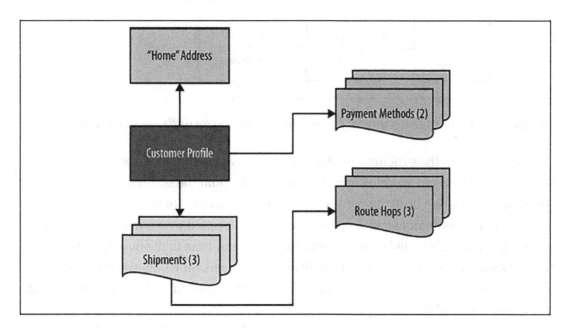

Figure 3-1. *Data model for Shipping Company using the "current state" approach*

The corresponding events-based model is shown in Figure 3-2.

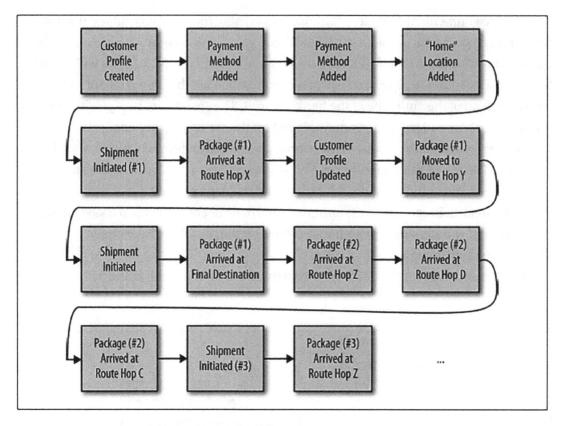

Figure 3-2. *Flow of Data model for Shipping Company with event sourcing*

As you can see, the structural model strives to only save the current state of the system, while the event sourcing approach saves individual "facts." State, in event sourcing, is a function of all the pertinent facts that occurred. Not only does this give you full auditability (as demonstrated in the case when you called your bank to dispute the balance), you can also build state projections toward any time in the past, not just the "now." Would you like to know where all the packages were on Wednesday? No problem with event sourcing! Answering this question would be more difficult with the structural model, since it would require special coding.

If you enjoy noticing patterns in seemingly unrelated things the way we do, we urge you to take another look at the two diagrams. You may notice how every entity in the structural model is a "snowflake" (i.e., it has a unique "shape," in terms of properties and relationships and was attentively crafted to represent differing real-life concepts).

In contrast, events in an event store all look the same from the outside. This is a very similar view to another technology closely related to microservices: containers. Indeed, for the container host (e.g., a Docker host), all containers look alike—the host doesn't "care" what is inside a container, it knows how to manage the lifecycle of a container independent of the contents of the container. In contrast, custom-installed enterprise applications have all kinds of peculiar "shapes" and environmental dependencies that the host must ensure exist (e.g., shared libraries the application expects).

The "indifference to shape and contents" approach seems to be a trend in modern technologies, as we can see the same pattern in SQL versus NoSQL storage. It is very reminiscent, in its tendency to show up under multiple contexts, of the "batch-size reduction" trend we noticed earlier while looking at different modern methodologies across multiple disciplines (e.g., project management, product development, operations, and architecture). We love this—when the same pattern emerges in multiple places, we can use our understanding of the pattern to identify or predict "next big thing."

But let's get back to microservices. You dipped your toes in a data-modeling technology called event sourcing and noted some of its benefits compared to conventional, structural modeling, but how exactly does it help you solve the data isolation and encapsulation challenges of microservice architecture? As it turns out, you need one more design pattern, CQRS, to complement event sourcing and you will be well on your way toward being able to design effective data storage for microservices with data persistence models that can avoid data sharing at even very small microservice sizes.

System Model for Shipping Company

As noted earlier, a good start for a microservice system design is to identify bounded contexts in the system. Figure 3-3 shows a context map for key bounded contexts in this problem space.

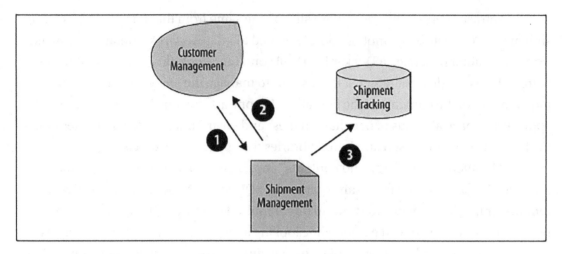

Figure 3-3. *High-level context map for the Shipping Company microservice architecture*

What are the capabilities of the three contexts and some of the data flows between the contexts, depicted by the arrows and numbers on the graph? They are as follows:

1. Customer Management creates, edits, and enables/disables customer accounts, and can provide a representation of a customer to any interested context.

2. Shipment Management is responsible for the entire lifecycle of a package, from drop-off to final delivery. It emits events as the package moves through sorting and forwarding facilities, along the delivery route.

3. Shipment Tracking is a reporting application that allows end users to track their shipments on their mobile device.

If you were to implement a data model of this application using a traditional, structural, CRUD-oriented model, you would immediately run into data sharing and tight coupling problems. Indeed, notice that the Shipment Management and Shipment Tracking contexts will have to query the same tables, at the very least the ones containing the transitions along the route. However, with event sourcing, the Shipment Management bounded context (and its corresponding microservice) can instead record events/commands and issue event notifications for other contexts and those other contexts will build their own data indexes (projections), never needing direct access to any data owned and managed by the Shipment Management microservice.

The formal approach to this process is described in a pattern called CQRS.

CQRS

Command query responsibility segregation is a design pattern that states that you can (and sometimes should) separate data-update versus data-querying capabilities into separate models. It tracks its ancestry back to a principle called command–query separation CQRS takes this concept a large step further, instructing you to use entirely different models for updates versus queries. This seemingly simple statement often turns out to be powerful enough to save the day, especially in the complicated case of the reports-centric microservices we mentioned earlier in this chapter.

Since reports usually need to aggregate and contrast data generated in different parts of a large system, they often need to span multiple subsystems and bounded contexts and almost always require access to data from multiple contexts. But it is only so if you assume you have a single model for any entity, where you both query and update the entity. If you instead use CQRS, the need to access data across multiple contexts (and related problems) can be eliminated. With CQRS, the Shipment Management microservice can "own" and encapsulate any updates related to package delivery, just notifying other contexts about events occurring. By subscribing to notifications of these events, a reporting service such as Shipment Tracking can build completely independent, query-optimized models that don't need to be shared with any other service.

As you can see in Figure 3-4, thanks to CQRS, you are able to separate the data models of the Shipment Management and Tracking microservices. In fact, Shipping Management doesn't even need to know about the existence of the Tracking microservice, and the only thing the Tracking microservice relies on is a stream of events to build its query index. During runtime the Tracking microservice only queries its own index. Furthermore, the Tracking microservice can include event and command data from other microservices using the same flow, keeping its independence and loose coupling.

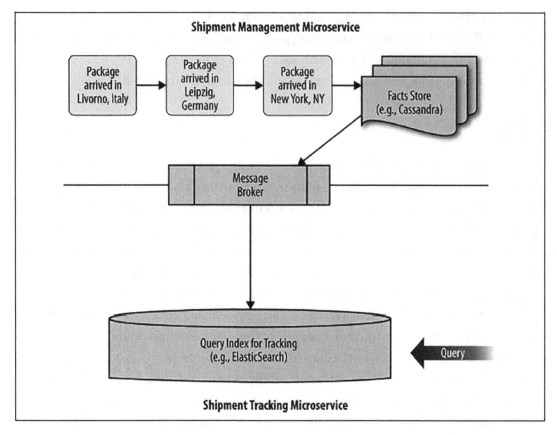

Figure 3-4. *Data flow in command-query responsibility segregation (CQRS)-based model for Shipping Company*

The big win with using event sourcing and CQRS is that they allow you to design very granular, loosely coupled components. With bounded contexts, the boundaries have to align with business capabilities and subdomain boundaries. With event sourcing, you can literally create microservices so tiny that they just manage one type of event or run a single report. Targeted use of event sourcing and CQRS can take you to the next level of autonomous granularity in microservice architecture. As such, they play a crucial role in the architectural style.

Do not overuse event sourcing and CQRS. You should only use event sourcing and CQRS when necessary, since they will complicate your implementation. Event sourcing and CQRS are not an "architecture" for your entire system, rather they are a powerful toolset to be used sparingly. There is still many use cases in which the conventional, CRUD-based model is much simpler and should be preferred.

Distributed Transactions and Sagas

The shared data model is not the only use case that can introduce tight coupling between microservices. Another important threat is workflows. A lot of real-life processes cannot be represented with a single, atomic operation, since they are a sequence of steps. When you are dealing with such workflows, the result only makes sense if all the steps can be executed. In other words, if any step in the sequence fails, the resulting state of the relevant system becomes invalid. You probably recognize this problem from RDBMS systems, where such processes are called "transactions." However, database transactions are local, contained within the confines of a single database where their implementations predominantly rely on the use of a shared state (i.e., you put locks on the rows and tables that participate in a transaction, guaranteeing data consistency). Once the transaction is fully executed you can remove the locks, or if any step of the transaction steps fails, you can roll back the steps already attempted.

For distributed workflows and share-nothing environments (and microservice architecture is both of those), you cannot use traditional transaction implementations with data locks and ACID compliance, since such transactions require shared data and local execution. Instead, an effective approach many teams use is known as "sagas". Sagas were designed for long-lived, distributed transactions by Hector Garcia-Molina and Kenneth Salem, and introduced in 1987 (yes, way before microservices or even the Web) during their work at Princeton University.

Sagas are very powerful because they allow running transaction-like, reversible workflows in distributed, loosely coupled environments without making any assumptions on the reliability of each component of the complex system or the overall system itself. The compromise here is that sagas cannot always be rolled back to the exact initial state of the system before the transaction attempt. But you can make a best effort to bring the system to a state that is consistent with the initial state through compensation.

In sagas, every step in the workflow executes its portion of the work, registers a callback to a "compensating transaction" in a message called a "routing slip," and passes the updated message down the activity chain. If any step downstream fails, that step looks at the routing slip and invokes the most recent step's compensating transaction, passing back the routing slip. The previous step does the same thing, calling its predecessor compensating transaction and so on until all already executed transactions are compensated. for example: let's say a customer mailed a prepaid cashier's check for $100 via Shipping Company's insured delivery. When the courier showed up at the destination, they found out that the address was wrong and the resident wouldn't accept the package.

Thus, Shipping Company wasn't able to complete the transaction. Since the package was insured, it is Shipping Company's responsibility to "roll back" the transaction and return the money to the sender. With ACID-compliant transactions, Shipping Company is supposed to bring the exact $100 check back to the original sender, restoring the system state to its exact initial value. Unfortunately, on the way back the package was lost. Since Shipping Company. could no longer "roll back" the transaction, they decided to reimburse the insured value of $100 by depositing that amount into the customer's account. Since this was an active, long-time Shipping Company. customer and a rational human being, they didn't care which $100 was returned to them. The system didn't return to its exact initial state, but the compensating transaction brought the environment back to a consistent state. This is basically how sagas work.

Due to its highly fault-tolerant, distributed nature, sagas are very well-suited to replace traditional transactions when transactions across microservice boundaries are required in a microservice architecture. If you want to learn more about sagas and see working code implementing a very expressive example, refer to the link `https://docs.microsoft.com/en-us/azure/architecture/reference-architectures/saga/saga`

Asynchronous Message-Passing and Microservices

Asynchronous message-passing plays a significant role in keeping things loosely coupled in a microservice architecture. You probably noticed that in one of the examples earlier in this chapter, we used a message broker to deliver event notifications from our Shipment Management microservice to the Shipment Tracking microservice in an asynchronous manner. That said, letting microservices directly interact with message brokers (such as RabbitMQ, etc.) is rarely a good idea. If two microservices are directly communicating via a message-queue channel, they are sharing a data space (the channel), which you have learned is not a good idea. Instead, what you can do is encapsulate message-passing behind an independent microservice that can provide message-passing capability, in a loosely coupled way, to all interested microservices.

The message-passing workflow you are most interested in, in the context of microservice architecture is a simple publish/subscribe workflow. How do you express it as an HTTP API/microservice in a standard way? We recommend basing such a workflow on an existing standard, such as PubSubHubbub. Now to be fair, PubSubHubbub wasn't created for APIs or hypermedia APIs, it was created for RSS and Atom feeds in the blogging context. That said, you can adapt it relatively well to serve a hypermedia API-enabled workflow. To do so, you need to implement a flow like the one shown in Figure 3-5.

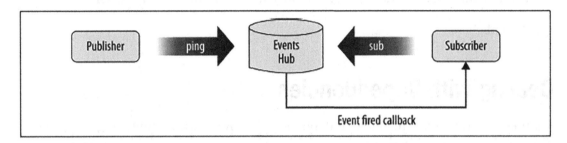

Figure 3-5. *Asynchronous message-passing implemented with a Pub-Sub-Hub-Bub inspired flow*

You also need to standardize some hypermedia affordances:

This refers to a hub that enables registration for notification of updates to the context:

```
rel="hub"
```

This gives the address of the pingback resource for the link context:

```
rel="pingback"
```

When included in a resource representation of an event, the "sub" (subscription) link relation may identify a target resource that represents the ability to subscribe to the pub/sub event-type resource in the link context:

```
rel="sub"
```

When included in a resource representation of an event, the "unsub" (subscription cancellation) link relation may identify a target resource that represents the ability to unsubscribe from the pub/sub event-type resource in the link context.

```
rel="unsub"
```

This is a resource representation of a subscribable events:

```
rel="event"
```

This is a link to a collection resource representing a list of subscribe events:

```
rel="events"
```

Dealing with Dependencies

Another important topic related to independent deploy ability is embedding dependencies. Imagine that Shipping Company's currency rates microservice is being hammered by user queries and requests from other microservices. It would cost you much less if you hosted that microservice in a public cloud rather than on expensive servers of your corporate data center. But it doesn't seem possible to move the microservice to another host, if it stores data in the same SQL or NoSQL database system as all other microservices.

Note that data tables are not shared, just the installation of the database management system. It seems like the logical conclusion is that you cannot have any microservice share even the installation of a data storage system. Some may argue that a microservice needs to "embed" every single dependency it may require, so that the microservice can be deployed wherever and whenever, without any coordination with the rest of the system.

A strict requirement of full dependency embedding can be a significant problem, since for decades we have designed our architectures with centralized data storage, as shown in Figure 3-6.

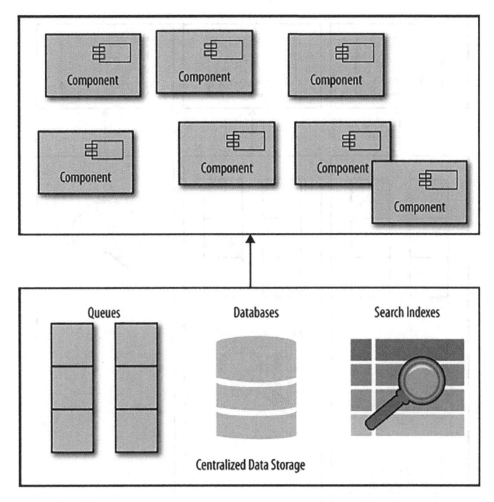

Figure 3-6. *Components using a centralized pool of dependencies*

Centralized data storage is operationally convenient: it allows dedicated, specialized teams (DBAs, sysadmins) to maintain and fine-tune these complex systems, obscuring the complexity from the developers.

In contrast, microservices favor embedding of all their dependencies, in order to achieve independent deployment. In such a scenario, every microservice manages and embeds its database, key-value store, search index, queue, and so on. Then moving this microservice anywhere becomes trivial. This deployment would look like Figure 3-7.

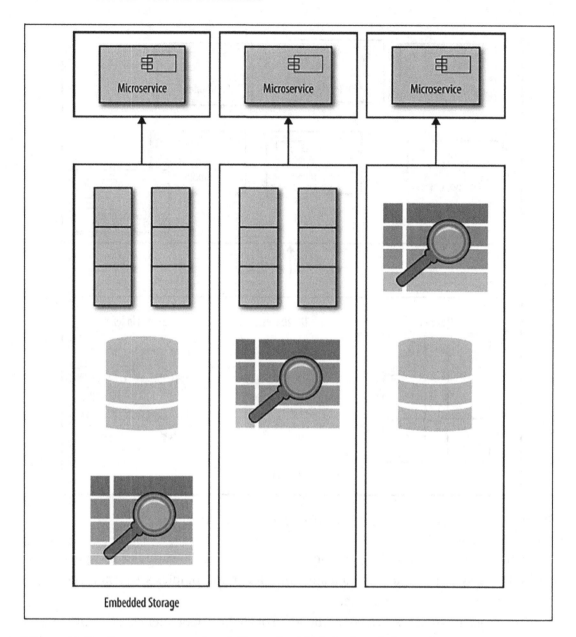

Figure 3-7. *Components using fully embedded, isolated dependencies*

The postulate of wholesale embedding of (data storage) dependencies looks beautiful on the surface, but in practice it is extremely wasteful for all but the simplest use cases. It is obvious that you will have a very hard time embedding entire Cassandra, Oracle, or Elasticsearch clusters in each and every microservice you develop. Especially if you are far down the microservices journey and possibly have hundreds of microservices. This is just not doable. Neither is it necessary.

A microservice doesn't have to carry along every single dependency (such as a data storage system) in order to be mobile and freely move across the data centers.

In his previous job, one of us (Irakli) traveled a lot for work. He'd acquired important tips for doing it efficiently—tips that he was completely indifferent to during his previous life as a casual traveler. As any frequent traveler will tell you, the most important rule for mobility is to keep your luggage light. You don't have to pack literally everything you may possibly need. For example, nobody packs shower-heads and towels on a business trip: you know you will find those at the hotel. If you know that the destination hotel has a convenience shop and your employer pays for incidentals, you don't even have to pack most toiletries. Irakli learned what he could count on being available "onsite" and what he needed to always bring with him. And, to pack light, he learned to limit his "dependencies" on a lot of things that were not needed as part of his packing routine.

Likewise, the trick to microservice mobility is not packing everything but instead ensuring that the deployment destination provides heavy assets, such as database clusters, in a usable and auto-discoverable form at every destination where a microservice may be deployed. Microservices should be written so that they can quickly discover those assets upon deployment and start using them.

To be clear: data sharing between microservices is still the ultimate no-no. Sharing data creates tight coupling between microservices, which kills their mobility. However, sharing a database cluster installation is okay, given that each microservice only accesses isolated, namespaced portions of it.

Pragmatic Mobility

Figure 3-8 shows what a proper, sophisticated microservices deployment should look like in practice.

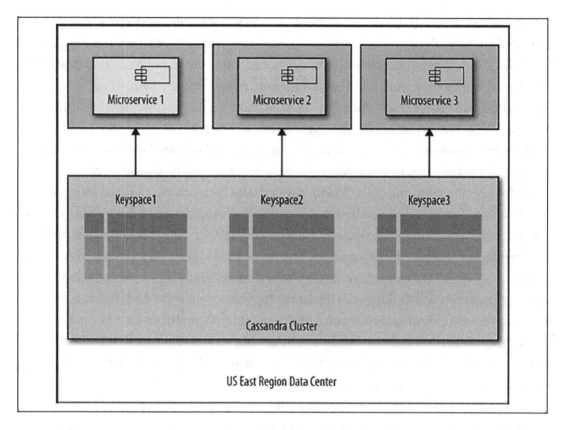

Figure 3-8. *Pragmatic approach: Components using a centralized pool of dependencies, without sharing data spaces*

If you decide to move Microservice 1 to another data center, it will expect that the new data center also has a functioning Cassandra cluster with a compatible version (in the earlier metaphor, the hotel provides towels you can use), but it will find a way to move its slice of data and won't depend on the existence or state of any other microservice at the destination, as mentioned in Figure 3-9.

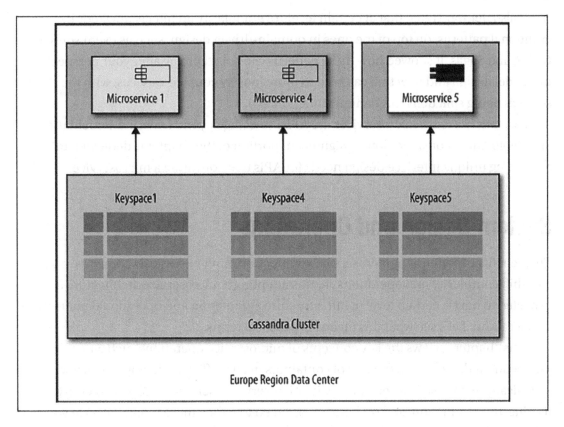

Figure 3-9. *Pragmatic approach: Microservice 1's move to different data center made possible without data sharing*

Microservices do not have to "travel" heavy and pack everything they may possibly require. In complex cases it is fine to have some reasonable expectations about the destination environment, especially when it comes to complex data-storage capabilities.

The most important question you need to ask, when deciding on embedding dependencies versus "expecting" traits in an environment, is will the decision increase or decrease mobility? The goal is to maximize deployment mobility of a microservice, which may mean different things in different contexts.

This chapter explained the overarching role of the "batch-size reduction" technique for systems engineering, when achieving both speed and safety at scale is the desired outcome.

It also demonstrated that at certain levels of granularity architects may require additional patterns, on top of the ones in domain-driven design, such as event sourcing, CQRS, and Sagas. It showed how these patterns can substantially alter your perspective on model design and how that can lead to more loosely coupled services, with the services being split delivering unique functionality.

Last, but not least, microservices are APIs, so going beyond code, implementation, and deployment considerations, a significant portion of the chapter is dedicated to explaining unique interface design needs for APIs that constitute a microservice.

System Design and Operations

The benefits of adopting a microservice architecture don't necessarily come free—they can shift complexity into operations. Teams adopting a microservice architecture are expected to have a certain level of infrastructure automation and operational maturity to be successful. Let's see what this means in practical terms.

This chapter reviews the key concepts of microservice operations such as independent deployment, the role of containers in cost-efficient deployments, and specifically, what role Docker can play in microservices, service discovery, security, routing, transformation, and orchestration. Taken together, these topics will give you a solid foundation for understanding, designing, and executing microservice architecture's operational needs.

Independent Deployability

One of the core principles of the microservice architectural style is the principle of independent deployability—that is, each microservice must be deployable completely independent of any other microservice. Some of the most important benefits of the architectural style rely on faithful adherence to this principle.

Independent deployment allows you to perform selective or on-demand scaling; if a part of the system (e.g., a single microservice) experiences high load, you can redeploy or move that microservice to an environment with more resources, without having to scale up hardware capacity for the entire, typically large, enterprise system. For many organizations, the operational ability of selective scaling can save large amounts of money and provide essential flexibility.

As a parcel-delivery company, Shipping Company needs to accept packages, route them through various sorting warehouses (hops on the route), and eventually deliver them to their destinations.

Let's consider an example of selective scaling for Shipping Company. This company stores and operates sensitive customer information including demographic and financial data for its customers. Shipping Company collects credit card information and, as such, falls under the auditing requirements of strict government regulation.

For security reasons, Shipping Company deploys sensitive parts of the implementation at an on-premise data center, but its CTO would still like to utilize "cloud computing," for cost and scalability reasons, when possible.

Scaling hardware resources on-premise can be extremely costly—you must buy expensive hardware in anticipation of the usage rather than in response to actual usage. At the same time, the part of the application that gets hammered under load and needs scaling may not contain any sensitive client or financial data. It can be something as trivial as an API returning a list of U.S. states or an API capable of converting various currency rates. The chief architect of Shipping Company is confident that their security team will easily allow deployment of such safe microservices to a public/ private cloud, where scaling of resources is significantly cheaper. The question is—could they deploy part of an application to a separate data center, a cloud-based one, in this case? The way most, typically monolithic, enterprise systems are architected, deploying selective parts of the application independently is either very hard or practically impossible. Microservices, in contrast, emphasize the requirement of independent deployment to the level of core principle, thus giving you much needed operational flexibility.

On top of operational cost saving and flexibility, another significant benefit of the independent deployment is an organizational one. Two different teams would be responsible for the development of separate microservices (e.g., Customer Management and Shipment Management). If the first team, which is responsible for the Customer Management microservice, needs to make a change and rerelease, but Customer Management cannot be released independent of the Shipment Management microservice, you now need to coordinate Customer Management's release with the team that owns Shipment Management. Such coordination can be costly and complicated, since the latter team may have completely different priorities from the team responsible for Customer Management. Often the necessity of such coordination will delay a release. Now imagine that, instead of just a handful, you potentially have hundreds of microservices maintained by dozens of teams. Release coordination overhead can be devastating for such organizations, leading to products that ship with significant delays or sometimes become obsolete by the time they can be shipped.

Do You Need More Servers?

To ensure independent deployment, you need to develop, package, and release every microservice using an autonomous, isolated unit of environment. But what does "autonomous, isolated unit of environment" mean in this context? What are some examples of such units of environment? Let's assume you are developing a service application. At first glance, something like *Service application file* may seem like an appropriate unit of encapsulation and isolation.

After all, that's what these packaging formats were designed for—to distribute a collection of executable code and related resources that together form an independent application, within the context of an application server.

Lightweight packaging solutions—such as NPM modules (for Node) or PIP packages (for Python)—don't provide enough modularity and the level of isolation required for microservices. Service deployment files still share system resources like disk, memory, shared libraries, the operating system, and so on. They may also expect specific versions of OS libraries in the environment. As any experienced sysadmin or DevOps engineer knows, one application's environmental expectations can be drastically different from another's, leading to version and dependency conflicts if you need to install both applications on the same server. One of the core motivations of adopting a microservice architecture is to avoid the need for complex coordination and conflict resolution, thus packaging solutions that are incapable of avoiding such interdependencies are not suitable for microservices. You need a higher level of component isolation to guarantee independent deployment.

What if you deployed a microservice per physical server or per virtual machine? Well, that would certainly meet the high bar of isolation demanded by microservices, but what would be the financial cost of such a solution? For companies that have been using microservice architecture for several years, it is not uncommon to develop and maintain hundreds of microservices. Let's assume you work at a mature microservices company with about 500 microservices. To deploy these microservices in a reliable, redundant manner you will need at least three servers/VMs per each microservice, resulting in

1,500 servers just for the production system. Typically, most companies run more than one environment (QA, stage, integration, etc.), which quickly multiplies the number of required servers.

Here comes the bad news: thousands of servers cost a lot. Even if you use VMs and not physical servers, even in the "cheapest" cloud-hosting environment the budget for a setup utilizing thousands of servers would be significantly high, probably higher than what most companies can afford or would like to spend. And then there's that important question of development environments. Most developers like to have a working, complete, if scaled down, model of the production environment on their workstations.

How many VMs can you realistically launch on a single laptop or desktop computer? Maybe five or ten, at most? Not hundreds or thousands. So, what does this quick, on-a-napkin-style calculation of microservices hosting costs mean? Is a microservice architecture simply unrealistic and unattainable, from an operational perspective? It probably was, for most companies, some number of years ago. And that's why you see larger companies, such as Amazon and Netflix, being the pioneers of the architectural style—they were the few who could justify the costs.

Things, however, have changed significantly in recent years.

Microservice Architecture Is a Product of Its Time

We often get asked—what is the fundamental difference between microservice architecture and service-oriented architecture, especially given that so many underlying principles seem similar? We believe that the two architectural styles are creations of their respective eras, roughly a decade apart. In those 10 years the industry has gotten significantly more skilled in effective ways of automating infrastructure operations. Microservice architecture is leveraging the most advanced achievements in DevOps and continuous delivery, making the benefits of the architectural style available and cost-effective to much wider audiences than just a handful of large early adopters like Amazon or Netflix.

The reason microservice architecture is financially and operationally feasible has a lot to do with containers.

The deployment unit universally used for releasing and shipping microservices is a container. If you have never used containers before, you can think of a container as of an extremely lightweight "virtual machine." The technology is very different from that of conventional VMs. It is based on a Linux kernel extension (LXC) that allows running many isolated Linux environments (containers) on a single Linux host sharing the operating system kernel, which means you can run hundreds of containers on a single server or VM and still achieve the environment isolation and autonomy that is on par with running independent servers, and is therefore entirely acceptable for our microservices needs.

Containers will not be limited to just Linux; there are containers now coming from Microsoft Windows to be deployed .Containers provide a modern isolation solution with practically zero overhead. While you cannot run more than a handful of conventional VMs on a single host, it is completely possible to run hundreds of containers on a single host. Currently the most widely deployed container toolset is Docker, so in practice Docker and containers have become somewhat synonymous. In reality, there are other up-and-coming container solutions, which may gain more prominence in the future.

Docker and Microservices

This section discusses Docker, as it is the container toolset most widely deployed in production today. However, as mentioned, alternative container solutions exist in varying stages of production readiness. Therefore, most things in this section should be understood as relevant to containers in general, not just Docker specifically.

At the beginning of 2016, most microservices deployments were practically unthinkable without utilizing Docker containers. We have discussed some of the practical reasons for this. That said, you shouldn't think of Docker or containers as tools designed just for the microservice architecture.

Containers in general, and Docker specifically, certainly exist outside microservice architecture. As a matter of fact, if you look at the current systems operations landscape you can see that the number of individuals and companies using containers many times exceeds those implementing microservice architecture. Docker in and of itself is significantly more common than the microservice architecture.

Containers were not created for microservices. They emerged as a powerful response to a practical need: technology teams needed a capable toolset for universal and predictable deployment of complex applications. Indeed, by packaging the application as a Docker container, which assumes pre-bundling all the required dependencies at the correct version numbers, you can enable others to reliably deploy it to any cloud or on-premise hosting facility, without worrying about target environment and compatibility.

The only remaining deployment requirement is that the servers should be Docker-enabled, in most cases. In comparison, if you just gave somebody your application as an executable, without pre-bundled environmental dependencies, you would be setting them up for a load of dependency pain. Alternatively if you wanted to package the same software as a VM image, you would have to create multiple VM images for several major platforms, since there is no single, dominant VM standard currently adopted by major players.

But compatibility is not the only win; there's another benefit that is equally, if not more, important when you consider containers versus VM images. Linux containers use a layered filesystem architecture known as *union mounting*. This allows a great extensibility and reusability not found in conventional VM architectures. With containers, it is trivial to extend your image from the "base image." If the base image updates, your container will inherit the changes at the next rebuild. Such a layered, inheritable build process promotes a collaborative development, multiplying the efforts of many teams. Centralized registries, discovery services, and community oriented platforms such as Docker Hub and GitHub further facilitate quick adoption and education in the space.

As a matter of fact, we could easily turn the tables and claim that it is Docker that will be driving the adoption of microservices instead of vice versa. One of the reasons for this claim is that Docker puts significant emphasis on the "UNIX philosophy" of shipping containers, i.e., "do one thing, and do it well." Indeed, this core principle is prominently outlined in the Docker documentation itself:

Run only one process per container. In almost all cases, you should only run a single process in a single container. Decoupling applications into multiple containers makes it much easier to scale horizontally and reuse containers.

—Docker documentation

With such principles at its core, Docker philosophy is much closer to the microservice architecture than a conventional, large monolithic architecture. When you are shooting for "doing one thing" it makes little sense to containerize your entire, huge, enterprise application as a single Docker container. Most certainly you would want to first modularize the application into loosely coupled components that communicate via standard network protocols, which is what the microservice architecture delivers. As such, if you start with a goal of containerizing your large and complex application you will likely need a certain level of microservice design in your complex application.

The way we like to look at it, Docker containers and microservice architecture are two ends of the road that lead to the same goal of continuous delivery and operational efficiency. You may start at either end, if the desired goals are achieved.

The Role of Service Discovery

If you are using Docker containers to package and deploy your microservices, you can use a simple Docker Compose configuration to orchestrate multiple microservices (and their containers) into a coherent application. As long as you are on a single host (server) this configuration will allow multiple microservices to "discover" and communicate with each other. This approach is commonly used in local development and for quick prototyping.

But in production environments, things can get significantly more complicated. Due to reliability and redundancy needs, it is very unlikely that you will be using just one Docker host in production. Instead, you will probably deploy at least three or more Docker hosts, with several containers on each one of them.

Furthermore, if your services get significantly different levels of load, you may decide to not deploy all services on all hosts but end up deploying high-load services on a select number of hosts (let's say ten of them), while low-load services may only be deployed on three servers, and not necessarily the same ones. Additionally, there may be security- and business-related reasons that may cause you to deploy some services on certain hosts and other services on different ones.

In general, how you distribute your services across your available hosts will depend on your business and technical needs and very likely may change over time. Hosts are just servers, they are not guaranteed to last forever.

Each instance of the microservice container is with a different number. In this example, you have Microservice 1 deployed on all four hosts, but Microservice 2 is only on hosts 1–3. Keep in mind that the deployment topology may change at any time, based on load, business rules, which host is available, and whether an instance of your microservice suddenly crashes or not.

Note that since typically many services are deployed on the same host, you cannot address a microservice by just an IP address. There are usually too many microservices, and the instances of those can go up and down at any time. If you allocated an IP per microservice, the IP address allocation and assignment would become too complicated. Instead, you allocate an IP per host (server) and the microservice is fully addressed with a combination of:

- IP address (of the host)
- Port number(s) the service is available on the host

We already noted that the IPs a microservice is available at are ever-changing, but what about the port? You might assume that you can assign fixed ports to individual microservices, saying, "our account management microservice always launches on port 5555." But this would not be a good idea. Many different teams will need to independently launch microservices on, likely, a shared pool of hosts. If you assumed that a specific microservice always launches on a specific port of a host, you would require a high level of cross-team coordination to ensure that multiple teams don't accidentally claim the same port. But one of the main motivations of using a microservice architecture is eliminating the need for costly cross team coordination. Such coordination is untenable, in general. It is also unnecessary since there are better ways to achieve the same goal.

This is where service discovery enters the microservices scene. You need some system that will always keep an eye on all services and keep track of which service is deployed on which IP/port combination at any given time, so that the clients of microservices can be seamlessly routed accordingly.

As mentioned in previous chapters, there are several established solutions in the open source space for service discovery. On one side of the spectrum are tools such as etcd from CoreOs and Consul by HashiCorp. They are "low-level" tools providing a high degree of control and visibility to an architect. On the other side of the spectrum are tools that provide "container-scheduling" capabilities, alongside the service discovery.

Kubernetes from Google is probably the most well-known in this category, Docker Swarm being another, more recent player. With container-scheduling solutions, you get a high degree of automation and abstraction. In this scenario, instead of deciding which container is launched on which servers, you just tell the system how much of the host pool's resources should be devoted to a service and Kubernetes or Swarm takes care of balancing/rebalancing containers on the hosts, based on these criteria. Another important technology utilizing containers is Mesosphere.

Mesosphere is even more abstracted than Kubernetes or Swarm, currently marketed as "a data center operating system" that allows a higher degree of automation, without having to worry about the many nodes deployed, and operating the entire server cluster.

There are no "better" tools when considering service discovery. As an architect, you need to decide how much automation "magic" you want from these tools versus how much control you need to retain for yourself. Even within the same enterprise application, it is very likely that you may find Kubernetes a great fit for a certain batch of microservices, whereas architects may decide that another class of microservices can be better deployed if directly managed using something like Consul.

The Need for an API Gateway

A common pattern observed in virtually all microservice implementations is teams securing API endpoints, provided by microservices, with an API gateway. Modern API gateways provide an additional, critical feature required by microservices: transformation and orchestration. In most mature implementations, API gateways cooperate with service discovery tools to route requests from the clients of microservices.

Security

Microservice architecture is an architecture with a significantly high degree of freedom. Or in other words, there are a lot more moving parts than in a monolithic application. As mentioned earlier, in mature microservices organizations where the architecture is implemented for complex enterprise applications, it is common to have hundreds of microservices deployed. Things can go horribly wrong security wise when there are many moving parts. You certainly need some law and order to keep everything in control and safe. Which is why, in virtually all microservice implementations, you see API endpoints provided by various microservices secured using a capable API gateway.

APIs provided by microservices may call each other, may be called by "frontend," i.e., public-facing APIs, or they may be directly called by API clients such as mobile applications, web applications, and partner systems. Depending on the microservice itself, the business needs of the organization, and the industry, market, or application context—all scenarios are fair game. To make sure you never compromise the security of the overall system, the widely recommended approach is to secure invocation of "public-facing" API endpoints of the microservices-enabled system using a capable API gateway.

Based on our experience building microservices systems and helping a wide variety of organizations do the same, we recommend a more radical approach than just securing "public API endpoints."

The distinction between "public" and "private" APIs often ends up being arbitrary. How certain are you that the API you think is "only internal" will never be required by any outside system? As soon as you try to use an API over the public Web, from your own web application or from a mobile application, as far as security is concerned, that endpoint is "public" and needs to be secured. The big picture for Amazon was with Amazon Web Services: they exposed the lowest level of the technical stack possible— hardware resources such as disk, CPU, networking etc., used by their ecommerce website—for anybody in the world to use and they made billions out of it.

So, why would you ever assume that you have some APIs that will forever be "internal only"? Sometimes, certain microservices are deemed "internal" and excluded from the security provided by an API Gateway, as you assume that they can never be reached by external clients. This is dangerous since the assumption may, over time, become invalid.

It's better to always secure any API/microservice access with an API gateway. In most cases the negligible overhead of introducing an API gateway in between service calls is well worth the benefits.

Transformation and Orchestration

As mentioned, microservices are typically designed to provide a single capability. They are the Web's version of embracing the UNIX philosophy of "do one thing, and do it well." However, as any UNIX developer will tell you, the single responsibility approach only works because UNIX facilitates advanced orchestration of its highly specialized utilities, through universal piping of inputs and outputs. Using pipes, you can easily combine and chain UNIX utilities to solve nontrivial problems involving sophisticated process workflows. A critical need for a similar solution exists in the space of APIs and microservices as well. Basically, to make microservices useful, you need an orchestration framework like UNIX piping, but one geared to web APIs.

Microservices, due to their narrow specialization and typically small size, are very useful deployment units for the teams producing them. That said, they might not be as convenient for consumption, depending on the client. The Web is a distributed system. Due to its distributed nature, on the Web, so-called "chatty" interfaces are shunned. Those are interfaces where you need to make many calls to get the data required for a single task. This distaste for chatty interfaces is especially pronounced among mobile developers, since they often must deal with unreliable, intermittent, and slow connections. There are a few things a mobile developer loathes more than an API interface that forces them to make multiple calls to retrieve something they consider a single piece of information.

Let's imagine that after successful completion of the APIs required for the mobile application, the technical team behind Shipping Company's microservice architecture decided to embark on a new journey of developing an "intelligent" inventory management system. The purpose of the new system is to analyze properly anonymized data about millions of shipments passing through Shipping Company, combine this insight with all the metadata that is available on the goods being shipped, determine behavioral patterns of the consumers, and—utilizing human and machine algorithms— design a "recommendation engine" capable of suggesting optimal inventory levels to Shipping Company's "platinum" customers. If everything works, those suggestions will be able to help customers achieve unparalleled efficiency in managing product stock, addressing one of the main concerns of any online retailer.

If the team is building this system using a microservice architecture, they could end up creating two microservices for the main functionality:

1. Recommendations microservice, which takes user information in and responds with the list containing the recommendations—i.e., suggested stock levels for various products that this customer typically ships.

2. Product metadata microservice, which takes in an ID of a product type and retrieves all kinds of useful metadata about it.

Such separation of concerns, into specialized microservices, makes complete sense from the perspective of the API publisher, or as you may call them, the server-side team. However, for the team that is implementing the end-user interface, calling the preceding microservices is nothing but a headache. More likely than not, the mobile team is working on a user screen where they are trying to display several upcoming suggestions.

Let's say the page size is 20, so 20 suggestions at a time. With the current, verbatim design of the microservices, the user-interface team will have to make 21 HTTP calls: one to retrieve the recommendations list and then one for each recommendation to retrieve the details, such as product name, dimensions, size, price, and so on.

At this point, the user-interface team is not happy. They wanted a single list; but instead are forced to make multiple calls (the infamous "N+1 queries" problem, resurfaced in APIs). Additionally, the calls to the Product Metadata microservice return too much information (large payload problem), which is an issue for, say, mobile devices on slow connections. The result is that the rendering of the all-important mobile screen is slow and sluggish, leading to a poor user experience.

Scenarios like the one just described are all too common. As a matter of fact, they existed even before the dawn of the microservice architecture. For instance, the REST API style has been criticized a lot for "chatty interface." You do not have to build your microservice APIs in the RESTful style, but a similar problem still exists, since we decided that microservices need to do "one thing," which can lead to chattiness.

Fortunately, since the "chattiness" problem in the APIs is not new, mature API gateways are perfectly equipped to deal with the problem. A capable API gateway will allow you to declaratively, through configuration, create API interfaces that can orchestrate backend microservices and "hide" their granularity behind a much more developer-friendly interface and eliminate chattiness. In the example scenario, you can quickly aggregate the N+1 calls into a single API call and optimize the response payload. This gives mobile developers exactly what they need: a list of recommendations via a single query, with exactly the metadata they required. The calls to backend microservices will be made by the API gateway. Good API gateways can also parallelize the 20 calls to the Product Metadata microservice, making the aggregate call very fast and efficient.

Routing

The chapter already mentioned that in order to properly discover microservices, you need to use a service discovery system. Service discovery systems such as Consul and etcd will monitor your microservice instances and track metadata about what IPs and ports each one of your microservices is available at, at any given time. However, directly providing tuples of the IP/port combinations to route an API client is not an adequate solution. A proper solution needs to abstract implementation details from the client.

An API client still expects to retrieve an API at a specific URI, regardless of whether there's a microservice architecture behind it and independent of how many servers, Docker containers, or anything else is serving the request.

Some of the service discovery solutions (e.g., Consul, and etcd using SkyDNS) provide a DNS-based interface to discovery. This can be very useful for debugging, but still falls short of production needs because normal DNS queries only look up domain/IP mapping, whereas for microservices you need domain mapping with an IP +port combination. In both Consul and SkyDNS, you can use DNS to look up both IP and port number, via an RFC 2782 SRV query, but realistically no API client expects or will appreciate having to make SRV requests before calling your API.

This is not the norm. Instead, what you should do is let an API gateway hide the complexities of routing to a microservice from the client apps. An API gateway can interface with either HTTP or DNS interfaces of a service discovery system and route an API client to the correct service when an external URI associated with the microservice is requested. You can also use a load balancer or smart-reverse proxy to achieve the same goal, but since you already use API gateways to secure routes to microservices, it makes a lot of sense for the routing requirement to also be implemented on the gateway.

Monitoring and Alerting

As mentioned, while microservice architecture delivers significant benefits, it is also a system with a lot more moving parts than the alternative—monolith. As such, when implementing a microservice architecture, it becomes very important to have extensive system-wide monitoring and to avoid cascading failures.

The same tools mentioned for service discovery can also provide powerful monitoring and failover capabilities. Let's take Consul as an example. Not only does Consul know how many active containers exist for a specific service, marking a service broken if that number is zero, but it also allows you to deploy customized health-check monitors for any service. This can be very useful. Indeed, just because a container instance for a microservice is up and running doesn't always mean the microservice itself is healthy. You may want to check that the microservice is responding on a specific port or a specific URL, possibly even checking that the health ping returns predetermined response data.

In addition to the "pull" workflow in which Consul agents query a service, you can also configure "push"-oriented health checks, where the microservice itself is responsible for periodically checking in, i.e., push predetermined payload to Consul. If Consul doesn't receive such a "check-in," the instance of the service will be marked "broken." This alternative workflow is very valuable for scheduled services that must run on predetermined schedules. It is often hard to verify that scheduled jobs do run as expected, but the "push"-based health-check workflow can give you exactly what you need.

These are powerful services that allow you to set up sophisticated incident-notification phone trees and/or notify your tech team via email, SMS, and push notifications through their mobile apps.

Summary

This chapter covered the various design principles used to derive microservices. You also saw the various patterns being used and learned how other companies like AWS and Netflix have created strong patterns that you can leverage for your microservices design and architecture.

You also looked at a practical example of patterns being implemented with the Shipping Company example.

The next chapter looks at the technology components like Docker and Kubernetes and explains how you can build such services and handle health monitoring.

Appendix

https://docs.microsoft.com/en-us/azure/architecture/reference-architectures/saga/saga

https://pubsubhubbub.appspot.com/

https://agilemanifesto.org/

CHAPTER 4

Containers and Azure Kubernetes Services

Introduction

So far, you have learned about the architectural and organizational considerations when assessing the maturity and readiness for microservices. You also looked at the design patterns used with microservices. This chapter explains containers and Azure Kubernetes Services, which form the foundational building blocks for microservices.

Containers

Containers form the foundational building blocks for building a scalable, platform-agnostic, and isolated hosting and processing ecosystem.

Containers are solution to the problem of how to get software to run reliably when it's moved from one computing environment to another—from a developer's machine to a test environment, from a staging environment into production, and perhaps from a physical machine to a data center to a virtual machine in a private or public cloud.

Problems arise when the supporting software environment is not identical. Maybe the software was tested using Python 2.7, and now it's going to run on Python 3 in production. Some weird behavior happens. The challenge is that you rely on the behavior of a certain version of an SSL library but another version is installed. You run your tests on one version of Linux and production is on Red Hat and all sorts of behavior changes are observed. Moving from one environment to another is unpredictable and involves a lot of effort trying to rectify the environment rather focusing on the actual work.

© Kasam Ahmed Shaikh and Shailesh S. Agaskar 2022
K. Ahmed Shaikh and S. S. Agaskar, *Azure Kubernetes Services with Microservices*,
https://doi.org/10.1007/978-1-4842-7809-3_4

How Containers Solve This Problem

Containers are of an entire runtime environment (i.e., the application, plus all its dependencies, libraries, other binaries, and configuration files needed to run it, all bundled into one package). By containerizing the application platform and its dependencies, differences in OS distributions and underlying infrastructure are abstracted away.

How Containerization Is Different from Virtualization

Virtualization technology is nothing but a package that is installed as a virtual machine, which includes an entire operating system and the application (see Figure 4-1). An actual physical server runs three virtual machines and would have a hypervisor and three separate operating systems running on top of it.

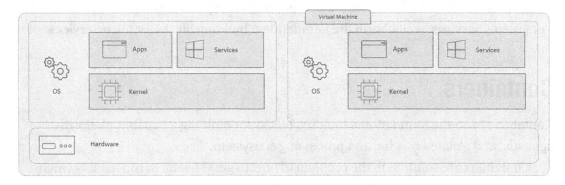

Figure 4-1. *Virtual machine architecture*

On the other hand, a server running three containerized applications with Docker runs a single operating system, and each container shares the operating system kernel with the other containers (see Figure 4-2). Shared parts of the operating system are read only, while each container has its own mount (i.e., a way to access the container) for writing. That means the containers are much more lightweight and use far fewer resources than virtual machines.

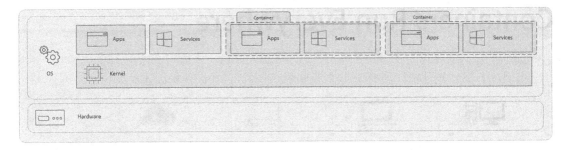

Figure 4-2. *Container architecture Courtesy: $https://docs.microsoft.com/ en-us/virtualization/windowscontainers/about/containers-vs-vm$*

The following benefits are derived from containerization:

- Isolation

- Compact

- Consistent

- Fast

- Simple

- Scalable

- Portable

Containers can run on various devices and operating systems, as illustrated in Figure 4-3.

Containers Run Everywhere

Figure 4-3. Containers run everywhere

The diagram in Figure 4-4 shows how traditional deployment has evolved to containers.

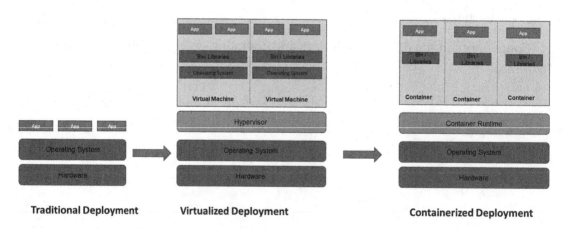

Figure 4-4. Evolution of deployments over time Courtesy: https://kubernetes.io/docs/concepts/overview/what-is-kubernetes/#going-back-in-time

There are two types of containers available—Linux and Windows—and the image layers are shown in Figure 4-5.

Image Layers

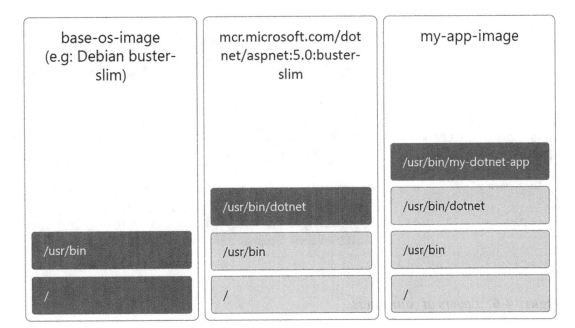

Figure 4-5. *Layers within the image*

The container layer is shown in Figure 4-6.

Container Layers

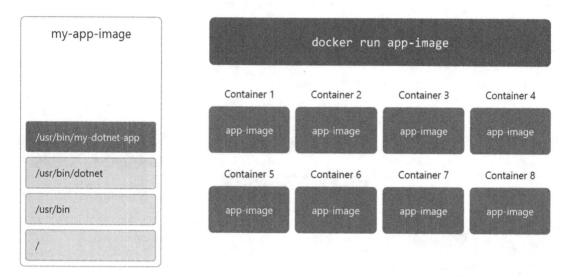

Figure 4-6. *Layers of containers*

Using Docker

Docker is an open platform for developing, shipping, and running applications. Docker enables you to separate your applications from your infrastructure so you can deliver software quickly. With Docker, you can manage your infrastructure in the same ways you manage your applications. See Figure 4-7.

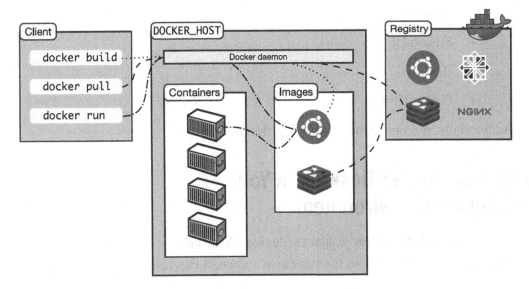

Figure 4-7. *Docker containers interaction Courtesy:* `https://docs.docker.com/`
`get-started/overview/`

The development tools for building docker containers are listed here:

- VS Code

- Recommended for Windows:

  - Windows Terminal

    - `https://github.com/microsoft/terminal#installing-`
      `and-running-windows-terminal`

  - Windows Subsystem for Linux (WSL2) if permitted

    - `https://docs.microsoft.com/en-us/windows/wsl/about`

  - Package Managers such as `winget` or `scoop` if permitted (make it
    easier to install CLI tools on Windows)

  - Preferred shell of your choice: PowerShell Core (pwsh), GitBash,
    WSL2 Bash/ZSH, and so on

- CLI Tools: Used to execute commands to run build and run Docker
  containers on Kubernetes services.

  - Git

  - Azure CLI

- Kubectl

- Kustomize

- Helm

- Curl or Httpie

Additionally, you need Docker Desktop, described next.

Installing Docker Desktop in Your Development Environment

See https://www.docker.com/products/docker-desktop.

First, make Sure Kubernetes is enabled, as shown in Figure 4-8.

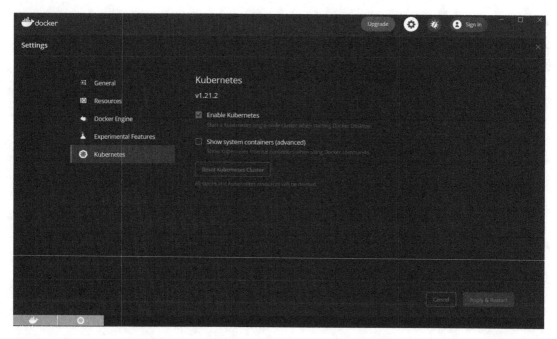

Figure 4-8. Kubernetes enabled settings

If you're using WSL2, don't forget to enable it to set limits, as explained at https://docs.microsoft.com/en-us/windows/wsl/wsl-config#configure-global-options-with-wslconfig. You also need to integrate Docker into your wsl2 distro (see the Resources option).

Let's now look at a basic level "Hello World" program to be deployed on Docker containers. If the Docker image is not already downloaded locally, Docker pulls it from the Docker Hub.

From the terminal, run the following:

```
docker run hello-world
```

Note   docker run = docker create + docker start (+ also docker attach)

Where did the hello-world image come from? Is it an official image?

Hint   See https://hub.docker.com/_/hello-world.

Observe the output log, starting by pulling the image from public registry.

Now you need to run Ubuntu and Interact with its shell environment:

```
docker run -it ubuntu bash
```

or

```
docker run -i -t ubuntu bash
```

Execute these commands inside the Docker container:

```
ls
```

Exit the container shell by typing exit.

Take your time to understand what the -it flag does when it's used with docker run:

```
`i` - keep STDIN open even if not attached
`t` - Allocate a pseudo-tty
```

One easy mnemonic to remember is that -it means *i*nteractive *t*erminal.

To view the locally cached images, use this command:

```
docker images
```

The result shows images that are locally cached in your environment. The next time you run that exact image, it won't be pulled from the registry.

Exploring the docker run Command

Run the same Ubuntu image again, but with a little twist this time:

1. Run it without bash at the end. Notice how it still works the same way as before? This is because the Ubuntu image's cmd is set to run bash by default. Exit the container shell.

    ```
    docker run -it ubuntu
    ```

Note   If you just run docker run ubuntu, bash will exit automatically as it does not have a stdin to listen to. You'll learn later about executing a process using EntryPoint in Docker and how web apps use it.

---

2. Now override the default cmd with some other command, such as ls. Run the following command and notice the different result:

    ```
    docker run -it ubuntu ls
    ```

Observe the result. What's going on here? You are overriding the default cmd for that image. See https://docs.docker.com/engine/reference/run/#cmd-default-command-or-options.

Running a Webserver

Run an nginx webserver as follows:

```
docker run -d -p 9000:80 nginx
# -p stands for publish (publish a container's port to the host)
```

You will be able to see the webpage on localhost:9000 if you are running docker locally or in a linux vm.

The -d flag indicates that the container will run in detached mode, so it's not waiting for input via stdin.

```
# See running containers
    docker ps
```

Now, run another instance of the nginx container. Just use a different port.

```
docker run -d -p 9001:80 nginx
docker ps # notice the new container from same image. Much like new objects
from a class.
```

Viewing the Contents of the Web Page from the Terminal

You can view the web page from a browser or a terminal using HTTP client tools such as curl or httpie:

```
curl localhost:9000

# or via httpie (for coloured output and more helpful info)
http localhost:9001
```

Now stop the nginx containers:

```
# run `docker ps` to list the running containers.

docker stop <container-id>
        or
docker stop <container_name_1> <container_name_2> # Note: it's container
name not image name.
```

Bonus: Look for the differences between the stop, kill, and rm commands.

Now you can see all containers, including the created and exited ones:

```
# `docker ps` only shows containers that are of status `Running`. To see
all containers, use `-a` flag

  docker ps -a
```

You can always start a stopped container by issuing the start command.

Find the container you want to start by looking it up on docker ps -a. Just because the container has stopped or exited, doesn't mean it's dead.

```
docker start <container_id or name>
```

Cleanup Processes

To remove a stopped container, use this command:

```
docker rm <container_id/name>
```

To remove images, use this command:

```
docker rmi image <image_id_1> <image_id_2>
```

Clean up dangling resources using the `docker system prune` command:

```
docker system prune
```

To clean up all resources, including images, containers, volumes, and so on, use this command:

```
docker system prune --all

# `y' when prompted
```

Important   As with any other system, use these clean up commands with caution. Do not force delete images that are still referenced by containers.

Give these links a quick read:

- https://docs.docker.com/engine/reference/commandline/
  system_prune/

- https://docs.docker.com/config/pruning/

- https://docs.docker.com/engine/reference/commandline/rmi/

To check if your environment is cleaned up, use these commands:

```
docker ps -a
docker images -a
```

The next section looks at Docker basics.

The Dockerfile

To begin this example, create a directory called Docker Directory. Create your first Dockerfile and execute a CMD (greeter:1.0):

1. From the docker directory, create a subdirectory called my_first_ dockerfile and create a Dockerfile inside it. The setup should be as shown here, so that you have a base directory called docker.

    You can use touch Dockerfile from the terminal or just right-click the appropriate folder and select New File:

```bash
  # from my_first_dockerfile directory
  touch Dockerfile
```

Your setup should look like this:

```bash
├── my_exercise
    ├── docker
    │   └── my_first_dockerfile
    │       └── Dockerfile
    └── kubernetes
```

2. Type the following inside the Dockerfile. (Avoid copying and pasting unless specified.)

    ```
    FROM ubuntu
    # Base Layer
    CMD ["echo", "Hello everyone"]
    ```

3. Build your Docker image. Make sure the terminal is pointing to the directory where the Dockerfile is located.

4. Build an image called greeter and tag it as version 1.0:

    ```
    docker build . -t greeter:1.0
    ```

5. Important: Take your time to understand what -t does. Also note the . (dot) after `docker build`.

6. View your new docker image using the `docker images` command.

7. Launch a container from the new Docker image:

```
docker run greeter:1.0
```

8. Observe the output and then make it print something by overriding the default CMD:

```
docker run greeter:1.0 echo "hello universe"
#or any command of your choice that is available in ubuntu image
docker run greeter:1.0 sleep "3"
```

Notice that you have to specify the full command to override the existing one.

Use Entrypoint to Make the Greeter a Bit More Configurable

1. Update the Dockerfile as shown next. Comment out the previously written code if needed.

```
FROM ubuntu

ENTRYPOINT [ "echo" ]

CMD ["Hello everyone"]
```

2. Build and tag the greeter image with version 2.0 and run the container.

```
docker build . -t greeter:2.0
docker run greeter:2.0
```

3. Now just run the following to make the container print the message of your choice.

```
docker run greeter:2.0 "Hello Greeter 2.0"
```

Use COPY to Launch a Simple Static Website

1. Create a new Dockerfile in another folder or feel free to continue working on your existing Dockerfile.

2. Create a folder called `website` and create a file inside called `index.html`. Type some simple markup, such as the following. Note that filenames in Linux are case sensitive.

   ```
   <h1>Hello World</h1>
   ```

3. Now, type the following into your Dockerfile:

   ```
   FROM nginx:alpine
   # Notice the change in base image.
   COPY ./website/ /usr/share/nginx/html
   ```

4. Copy the contents of website folder into the nginx default website location. Nginx is a powerful and highly popular webserver. See the Nginx base image at `https://hub.docker.com/_/nginx`.

5. Now build your Docker image as follows. Feel free to pick your own name for the image. Make sure your folder structure looks something like this before building:

   ```
   .
   ├── Dockerfile
   └── website
       └── index.html
       docker build . -t hello-web:1.0
       docker images "hello-web" # to see your new built image.
   ```

6. Run the image detached and do port-forwarding. You will get an exception if the port is already in use.

   ```
   docker run --name my-first-website -d -p 9000:80 hello-web:1.0
    # Notice the `--name` argument. We give our own container name
    this time.
   ```

7. Make sure that the container is running as expected with docker ps. Observe all the columns of your my-first-website container.

8. Stop the container using docker stop <container-name>.

Monitoring Docker Containers and Docker Logs

First start a container in detached mode that prints the date every second. We are using a busybox image here and calling the container date-printer:

```
docker run --name date-printer -d busybox sh -c "while true; do $(echo date); sleep 1; done"
```

Now follow its logs. Press Ctrl+C to exit.

```
docker logs -f date-printer
Retrieve logs only since last 3 seconds
docker logs date-printer --since=3s
```

See https://docs.docker.com/engine/reference/commandline/logs/.

Docker Exec: Run Commands Inside a Running Container!

Launch a redis container and be sure that it's running.

```
docker run -d redis
docker ps
# note down the container name
```

Now set some data with redis, using its CLI. First connect to its container shell.

```
docker exec -it <redis_container_name> sh
```

Once you're inside the container (when the prompt goes #), type the following:

```
redis-cli
```

The prompt should now look like 127.0.0.1:6379 (redis runs on 6379 by default):

```
set name "Jane"
exit
exit
# Exit from `redis-cli` and then from the `container shell`
```

From the terminal, you can directly retrieve that data. The following output should print Jane, for example:

```
docker exec -it <redis_container_name> redis-cli get name
```

Docker Inspect

You can inspect all the properties and states of a Docker object such as a container, network, volume, etc.

For example, to inspect a container, issue the following command:

```
docker inspect <container_id or name>
```

To inspect a Docker network, issue the following command:

```
docker network ls
docker inspect <network_name>
# for e.g: docker inspect bridge (default network that containers attach to
when network not specified)
```

With the Linux command-line tools such as jq, you can manipulate the JSON output. The following command will print the containers attached to the bridge network.

```
docker inspect bridge | jq '[.[].Containers]'
```

For more on jq, visit https://stedolan.github.io/jq/tutorial/.

Creating a Docker Hub Account and Connecting to It

Go to https://hub.docker.com/ and sign up using your temp/personal account. If you are using your personal email to sign up for Docker hub, make sure you're using your own personal dev machine. (you can also run docker logout when you're done).

1. Once you have created a Docker hub account, log in via the terminal, as follows:

    ```
    docker login
    ```

2. Enter your username and password when prompted. You should receive something like login succeeded.

Tagging and Pushing Your Image to the Registry

1. Before you can push your image to your registry, you need to tag it.

    Tag your hello-web image as shown here.

    ```
    docker images hello-web

    # Copy the image-id
    docker tag <image-id> <dockerhub-username>/hello-web:1.0

    docker push <docker-hub-username>/hello-web:1.0
    ```

2. Go to hub.docker.com to ensure your image is pushed correctly. You will come back to this image later during the Kubernetes labs.

3. You can always test your image by running it as follows.

    ```
    docker run -d -p 9010:80 <dockerhub-username>/hello-web:1.0
    docker ps
    docker stop <hello-web_container_id>
    ```

4. Log out of Docker hub from the terminal:

    ```
    docker logout
    ```

Clean up the resources as you did before to ensure your environment is correctly tidied up.

```bash
docker system prune -a
# type `y` when prompted
docker ps -a
docker images
```

Using Kubernetes

Now that you know how to run Docker Containers standalone, it's time to consider what happens when you have multiple containers to build and run. To enable that, you need an container orchestration engine like Kubernetes.

There are many container orchestrators, as listed here:

- Kubernetes

- Docker Swarm

- Mesos DC/OS

- Google Borg

- And many more

These orchestration engines provide the following features, which you don't have to build:

- Self-healing

- Load balancing

- Service discovery

- Scheduling

- Security

- Configuration

- Monitoring

- Scaling

The Kubernetes Architecture in a cloud is shown in Figure 4-9.

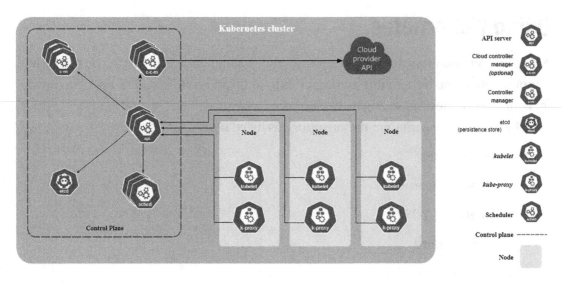

Figure 4-9. *Kubernetes architecture Courtesy:* https://kubernetes.io/docs/concepts/overview/components/

Figure 4-10 shows a deep dive into this architecture and illustrates how the components interact with each other.

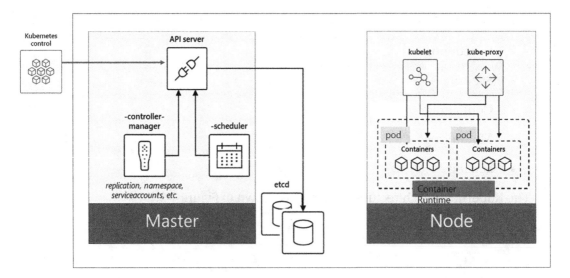

Figure 4-10. *Kubernetes components*

Running Kubernetes, you would need any of the following

- Minikube

- AKS (Azure Kubernetes Service)

- GKE (Google Kubernetes Engine)

- On-premise

- Raspberry Pi

- And many more

The key objects part of the overall Kubernetes framework are listed here:

- Nodes (no)

- Namespaces (ns)

- Pods (po)

- Deployments (deploy)

- Services (svc)

- Jobs

- Cronjobs

- Configmaps (cm)

- Secrets

- Persistentvolumeclaims (pvc)

- Persistentvolumes (pv)

Stateless microservices/apps on Kubernetes are shown in Figure 4-11.

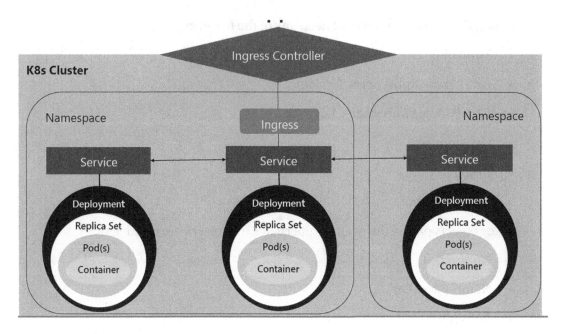

Figure 4-11. *Kubernetes deployments and replica sets*

Kubernetes Tooling and Setup

kubectl, pronounced *Kube-Control*, is the command-line interface for running commands against a Kubernetes clusters.

In this exercise, you will explore some features of kubectl that you may find useful.

1. Get cluster information:

   kubectl cluster-info

2. Write the cluster information to a file called cluster.txt. You may need bash/git-bash if the output stream > doesn't work:

   kubectl cluster-info > cluster.txt

3. You can also view it using cat if you like:

   cat cluster.txt

4. Get a list of all namespaces in the cluster. Here you will see other participant's namespaces too. In the real world, you might not have access to view other namespaces.

```
kubectl get namespaces
```

5. You can use the shorthand command as follows:

```
kubectl get ns
```

6. Filter your namespace using grep:

```
kubectl get ns | grep '<your-namespace-name>'
```

7. Check your default namespace for your current context:

```
kubectl config get-contexts
```

You should see your namespace under the NAMESPACE column.

Important   If the NAMESPACE column is blank or doesn't contain your namespace name, it means you haven't configured your default namespace correctly. See the repo's readme document or reach out to the instructor for help.

---

8. Get a list of nodes in the cluster:

```
kubectl get nodes
```

You can see more info with -o wide:

```
kubectl get nodes -o wide
```

kubectl explain will explain the given resource, such as a top-level API object like Pod or a specific field like a Pod's container.

1. Get the documentation of the Pod resource and its fields.

```
kubectl explain node
```

2.   Get the documentation for the Pod's container specification.

```
# to just explain pod
kubectl explain pod
# to further explain the properties and nested objects

kubectl explain pods.spec.containers
```

Note   pods.spec.containers matches the YAML object structure:

```
apiVersion: v1
kind: Pod
metadata:
creationTimestamp: null
name: nginx
spec:
  containers:
  - image: nginx
    imagePullPolicy: IfNotPresent
    name: nginx
    resources: {}
  dnsPolicy: ClusterFirst
  restartPolicy: Never
```

In the Azure portal, you can create the AKS clusters, as shown in Figure 4-12.

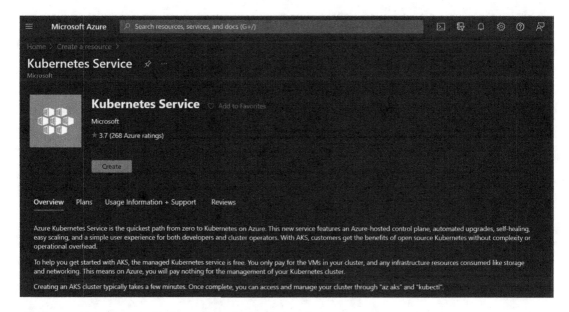

Figure 4-12. *Azure Kubernetes Service*

You click Create and then proceed with filling in the information based on your requirements. See Figure 4-13.

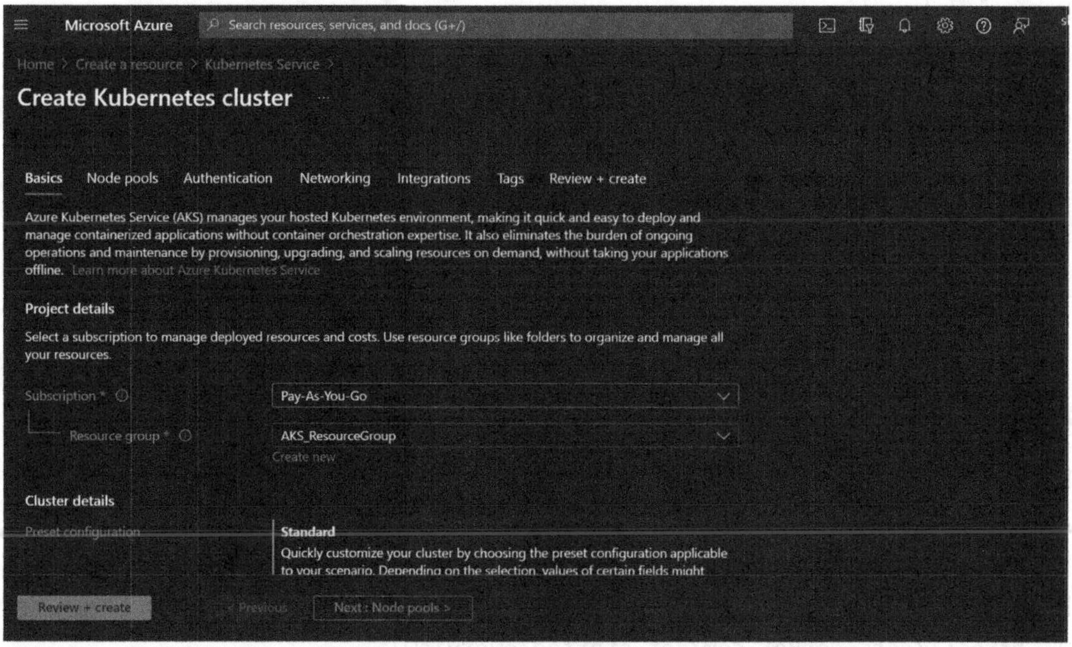

Figure 4-13. *Azure Kubernetes Service: Create Cluster*

Here are some of the high-level Azure CLI commands you can use:

Run `az --version` to find the version.

To create an Azure Kubernetes Cluster, issue the following command:

```
az aks create \
    --resource-group newResourceGroup \
    --name newAKSCluster \
    --node-count 3 \
    --generate-ssh-keys \
    --attach-acr <acrName>
```

To install the CLI, issue the following command:

```
az aks install-cli
```

To connect to the cluster, issue the following command:

```
az aks get-credentials --resource-group aksResourceGroup --name newAKSCluster
```

To get the nodes, issue the following command:

```
kubectl get nodes
```

Summary

In this chapter, you learned what containers and Kubernetes are and how to set up and use them in development. The next chapter looks at how to monitor and secure Azure Kubernetes Cluster (AKC).

Appendix

https://docs.microsoft.com/en-us/virtualization/windowscontainers/about/containers-vs-vm

https://kubernetes.io/docs/concepts/overview/what-is-kubernetes/#going-back-in-time

https://docs.docker.com/get-started/overview/

https://github.com/microsoft/terminal#installing-and-running-windows-terminal

https://docs.microsoft.com/en-us/windows/wsl/about

https://www.docker.com/products/docker-desktop

https://docs.microsoft.com/en-us/windows/wsl/wsl-config#configure-global-options-with-wslconfig

https://hub.docker.com/_/hello-world

https://docs.docker.com/engine/reference/run/#cmd-default-command-or-options

https://docs.docker.com/engine/reference/commandline/system_prune/

https://docs.docker.com/config/pruning/

https://docs.docker.com/engine/reference/commandline/rmi/

https://hub.docker.com/_/nginx

https://docs.docker.com/engine/reference/commandline/logs/

https://stedolan.github.io/jq/tutorial/

https://kubernetes.io/docs/concepts/overview/components/

CHAPTER 5

Securing and Monitoring Applications Running on AKS

Introduction

First, congratulations on completing 60 percent of this book. After reading about architecture designs and patterns, in this chapter, you'll go through another interesting and important aspect—monitoring and securing Azure Kubernetes service-based applications. You must be wondering why I didn't mention microservices. The answer is simple—when I say applications, that covers it all.

Digital platform initiatives are making organizations embrace the cloud culture. Cloud enablement includes building strategies to deliver more value to their clients. One of these strategies focuses on application security. With the growing pace of developments, it's important to plan the security of the applications to avoid any impediments in business operations.

Here, I present you with the security concepts for applications and clusters, concluding with one of the best reckoners for applications with respect to security.

© Kasam Ahmed Shaikh and Shailesh S. Agaskar 2022
K. Ahmed Shaikh and S. S. Agaskar, *Azure Kubernetes Services with Microservices*,
https://doi.org/10.1007/978-1-4842-7809-3_5

Security Concepts

Kubernetes and Microsoft Azure both include their respective security components. The Azure Kubernetes Service combines these security components to:

- Make sure your AKS Cluster is running the latest Kubernetes releases

- Ensure its up-to-date with OS security updates

- Secure Pod traffic

- Provide trusted access to sensitive credentials

Let's dive into a few core concepts for securing application and clusters in the Azure Kubernetes Service.

Master Security

In AKS, each cluster has a dedicated Kubernetes master-enabling API server, scheduler, and so on. This Kubernetes API sever uses an FQDN—a fully qualified domain name—along with a public IP address. As a PaaS service, Kubernetes Master components are included in managed services and are maintained by Microsoft.

You can adopt them in the following ways:

- You can create a private cluster, limiting server access to dedicated virtual networks.

- Using authorized IP ranges, you can restrict access to API server endpoints. Refer to Figure 5-1.

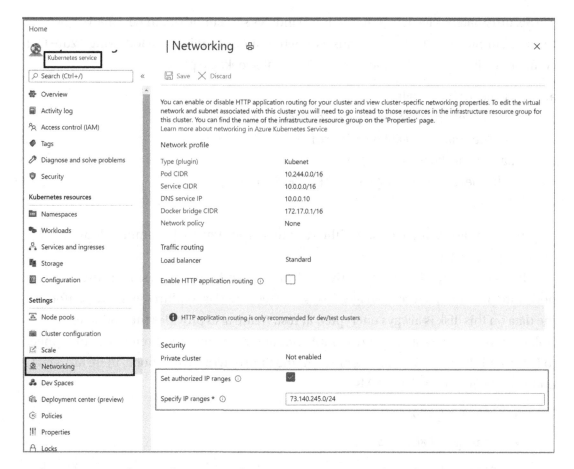

Figure 5-1. *Authorized IP range feature in Azure PortalImage source: Microsoft Documentation*

Also, you can control access by using Kubernetes RBAC and Azure RBAC. See the implementation details at https://docs.microsoft.com/en-us/azure/aks/managed-aad.

Node Security

Azure Kubernetes service nodes are nothing but the virtual machines that you manage. Linux and Windows server nodes both run an optimized Ubuntu distribution and Windows Server 2019 release respectively, using the Docker container runtime.

The latest OS security updates and configuration are deployed automatically on to nodes, whenever an AKS Cluster is created and also when it's scaled up.

Security patches for Linux nodes and Windows server nodes can be achieved by running simple azure CLI commands. For better understanding, the following Azure CLI command will upgrade the node pool called myaksbooknodepool:

```
az aks nodepool upgrade
    --resource-group myAKSBookResourceGroup \
    --cluster-name myAKSBookCluster \
    --name myaksbooknodepool \
    --kubernetes-version KUBERNETES_VERSION \
    --no-wait
```

This is just an example of one of the various simple Azure CLI commands available for managing nodes.

Nodes are always deployed to private virtual networks. Even the storage used by nodes are premium, Azure managed disks, backed by SSDs. Within the Azure platform, the data on this disk is always encrypted at rest. Azure also provides the option for isolated VMs, required as a part of compliance and regulatory requirements. This applies to Linux and Windows virtual machines. At the time of writing this book, there are a few options available for isolated VMs:

- `Standard_E80ids_v4`
- `Standard_E80is_v4`
- `Standard_F72s_v2`
- `Standard_M128ms`
- `Standard_DC8_v2`

Cluster Upgrades

An Upgrade Orchestration tool is provided by Azure, which includes the Kubernetes Master components and the Agent component. This tool enables the following actions:

- Upgrades of AKS Clusters and their components
- Security maintenance
- Compliance maintenance
- Access to the latest features

All it needs is the available Kubernetes version and the rest is taken care of, of course, with fewer commands.

Network Security

To communicate with your on-premises networks, you can have your AKS deployed to Azure virtual network subnets. Using Site-to-Site VPN or Express Route, this virtual network connects to your on-premises network. You can also define Kubernetes ingress controllers with private, internal IP addresses to limit services access to network connections. You can leverage Azure network security groups and even Kubernetes network policy to control the traffic flow.

Azure Kubernetes Service offers support to Kubernetes network polices, to limit network traffic between Pods in the given cluster based on namespaces, label selectors, and so on.

Kubernetes Secrets

With a Kubernetes Secret, you can add your sensitive data, such as access credentials and keys—to Pods. Use of Secrets minimizes the use of this sensitive information in (Pod or service YAML) manifests. You can request the secret as part of your manifest, limiting access to the information to specific Pods only.

Kubernetes secrets are stored in `Etcd`, a distributed key-value store. The `Etcd` store is fully managed by AKS and data is encrypted at rest within the Azure platform. See Figure 5-2.

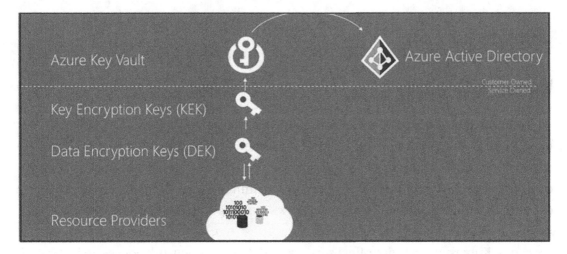

Figure 5-2. *Azure encryption at rest componentsImage source: Microsoft Documentation*

There are a few points you need to know about the Kubernetes Secrets:

- You can create a secret using the Kubernetes API.

- You define and request the secret for your Pod.

- Secrets are not written on disk, but are stored in `tmpfs`.

- When the Pod requiring the Secret is deleted, the secret is also deleted from the `tmpfs` nodes.

- Secrets are stored in a namespace, making them accessible only to the Pods within the same namespace.

Apart from these security concepts with respect to application and clusters, it's better to also go through the following:

- Azure security baseline for Azure Kubernetes Service

  (See `https://docs.microsoft.com/en-us/security/benchmark/ azure/baselines/aks-security-baseline?context=/azure/aks/ context/aks-context.`)

- Azure Policy Regulatory Compliance controls for Azure Kubernetes Service (AKS)

  (See `https://docs.microsoft.com/en-us/azure/aks/security- controls-policy.`)

Azure Kubernetes Service Checklist

This checklist contains some of the best practices to follow while working with AKS. It's not a kind of bible to follow, but simply best practices to adhere to when it comes to security

- **Refrain from injecting sensitive information into images and use Secrets instead**. As mentioned, avoid entering sensitive information like passwords directly into images or the manifest. Rather, always use Secrets—either Kubernetes Secrets or Azure Key Vaults—for such information. See Figure 5-3.

Figure 5-3. *Kubernetes Secrets and Azure KeyVault icons*

- **Implement Pod identity**. Don't have fixed credentials stored in Pod images. Rather you can use Pod identities, which use the Azure Identity solution for all the access to the desired (Azure) resources. These credentials could be any credentials used to talk with other Azure services, like Azure SQL or Azure Storage. You can define them in Kubernetes Secrets, but it needs a manual management. Here you can miss the best practice of rotating the Secrets being used.

Pod-managed identities for Azure resources can be used to have the access request via Azure AD. Figure 5-4 depicts the request flow.

Note   At the time of writing this book, Pod-managed identities for AKS is in preview.

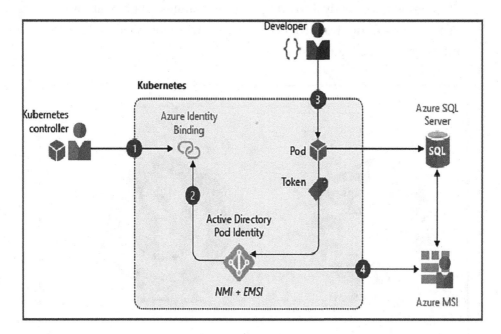

Figure 5-4. *A developer created a Pod that uses a managed identity to request access to an Azure SQL databaseImage source: Microsoft Documentation*

- **Use a Kubernetes Namespace**. Namespaces are the logical partitions of your resources. They not only enforce the separation of resources but also limit the permissible user scope. For simpler understanding, you can have different namespaces for different business units or groups. You should use the Kubernetes Namespace to isolate your Kubernetes resources. See Figure 5-5.

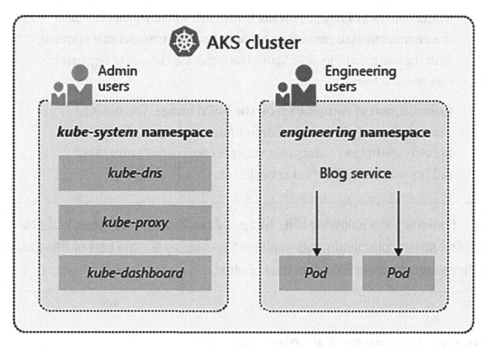

Figure 5-5. *Example of Namespaces in an AKS ClusterImage source: Microsoft Documentation*

The following namespaces are available when you create an AKS Cluster:

- `Default`: When no namespace is given, this is where Pods are created.

- `kube-system`: Where core resources exist.

- `kube-public`: These resources can be viewed by any user.

Important   Avoid using the default namespace.

- **Specifying the correct security context for a Pod**. This is an important factor in deciding your Pod access control settings. If the context is not set, the Pod gets the default one, which exposes it with more rights.

- **Manifest with best practices**. Ensure that the configuration of the manifest follows the best practices. A good manifest presents a good cluster. ☺

- **Static analysis of images on the build**. Introduce DevSecOps into the environment to promote a proactive security model that starts to shift the responsibility left. Azure Defender for container registries can be used here.

- **Enforcement of compliance on the build image**. You must go through Azure Policy built-in definitions for Azure Kubernetes Service; see `https://docs.microsoft.com/en-us/azure/aks/policy-reference?ref=akschecklist`.

Note   Bookmark the following URL: `https://www.the-aks-checklist.com/`. The seven commandments explained previously are the part of this forum, and they keep changing based on new context.

Security Concepts: Conclusion

AKS security aspects could be covered in an entire book of their own. However, considering the scope of this chapter, I tried to sum up things you should know when working with AKS-based applications. Consider these as answers you would expect from an interviewer panel, when discussing AKS-based application security.

The next section covers another important area, monitoring.

Monitoring Concepts

Your applications are secured but need to be up and available all the time. Securing applications that have no availability is useless. Hence, monitoring is an important area for you to be cognizant of. This section presents you with the details of monitoring AKS-based applications along with monitoring the AKS using Azure Monitor.

Container Insights

Resources that generate performance metrics and resource logs can be monitored for health and performance. Like other Azure resources, the Azure Kubernetes Service also has logs.

Azure Monitor has a feature called Container Insights that runs these checks for managed Kubernetes hosted with AKS. What makes it a favorite is its ability to present interactive views on data coming from different monitoring scenarios. It's natively integrated with Azure Kubernetes Service, helping to collect critical logs, send alerts, and visualize. Figure 5-6 shows Container Insights in Azure Portal.

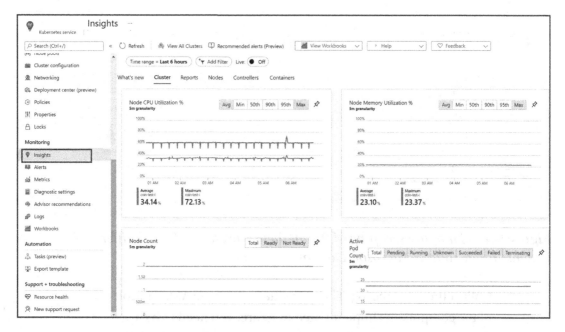

Figure 5-6. *Features of Container insightsImage source: Microsoft Documentation*

Here are the steps required to configure monitoring with Azure Monitor for an AKS Cluster:

1. Create a log analytics workspace. You must have one log analytics workplace to have telemetry data collected from the AKS Cluster. Container Insights requires at least one log analytics workplace.

2. Enable Container Insights. Enabling Container Insights depends on the AKS Cluster you are working on. Does the AKS Cluster already exist or is it a newly created one? Once enabled, a containerized version of the Log Analytics agent is deployed, which sends data to Azure Monitor.

3. Configure a collection from Prometheus. Using Container Insights allows you to collect Prometheus metrics without requiring a Prometheus server. This makes the combination successful for E2E monitoring. Refer to Figure 5-7, which depicts the working of Container Insights and Prometheus.

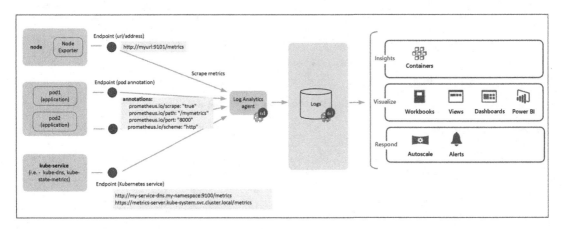

Figure 5-7. *Configure scraping of Prometheus metrics with Container InsightsImage source: Microsoft Documentation*

4. Collect the resource log. These are the logs for the AKS control plane components implemented in Azure. You need to have a diagnostic setting to collect these logs. You can have it in the log analytics workspace or in Azure storage. Figure 5-8 shows the screen for configuring diagnostics settings.

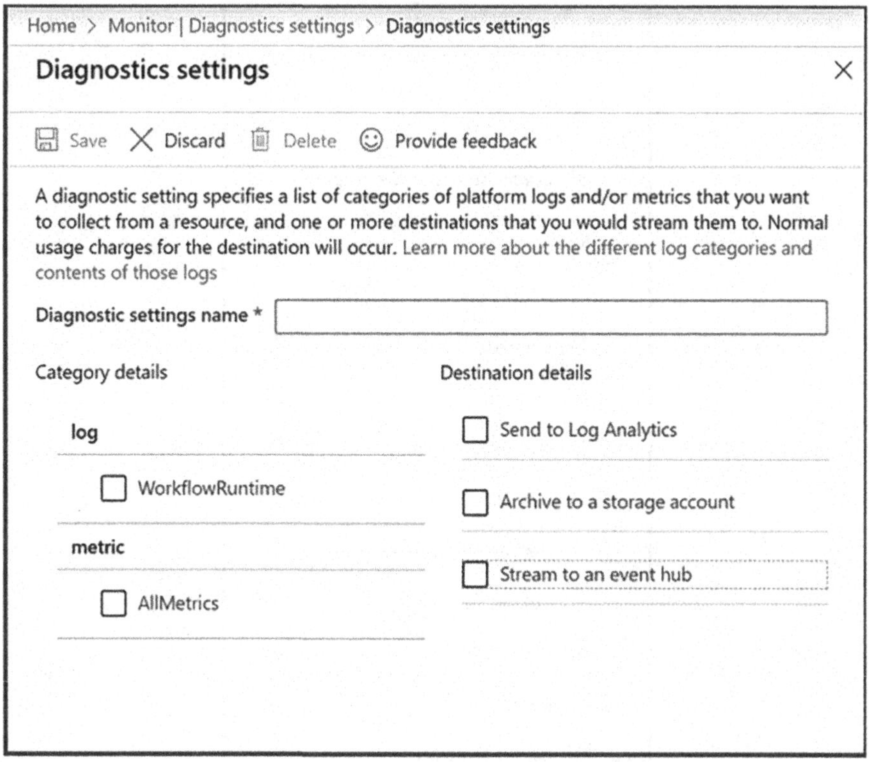

Home > Monitor | Diagnostics settings > Diagnostics settings

Diagnostics settings   ×

🖫 Save   ✕ Discard   🗑 Delete   ☺ Provide feedback

A diagnostic setting specifies a list of categories of platform logs and/or metrics that you want
to collect from a resource, and one or more destinations that you would stream them to. Normal
usage charges for the destination will occur. Learn more about the different log categories and
contents of those logs

Diagnostic settings name * [   ]

Category details   Destination details

   log   ☐ Send to Log Analytics

     ☐ WorkflowRuntime   ☐ Archive to a storage account

   metric   ☐ Stream to an event hub

     ☐ AllMetrics

Figure 5-8. *Screen for configuring diagnostics settings in Azure Portal*

Azure Monitor Features

There are two ways you can view the Azure Monitor features for AKS Clusters:

- Go to Azure Portal ➤ Kubernetes Service and choose the Monitor
  section from the left pane. This is mostly for single AKS Clusters.
  Refer to Figure 5-9.

Figure 5-9. *Insights option for the Kubernetes service screen in Azure Portal*

- Go to the Azure Portal. Type **Monitor** into the search box and then choose Insights Section ➤ Containers.

Figure 5-10 shows all the AKS Clusters in a subscription.

Figure 5-10. *Pane for Container Insights from the Monitor screen in Azure Portal*

Figure 5-11 is a fresh screen view for Monitor in Azure Portal. It is an entry point for monitoring clusters, creating alerts, and many more cool implementations.

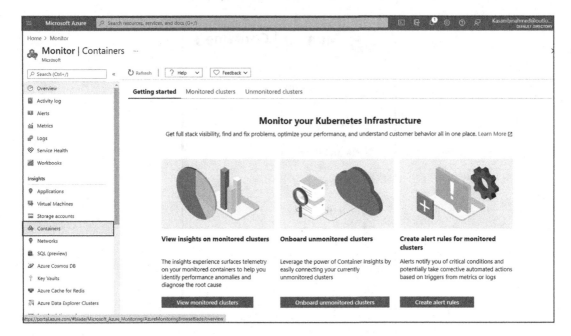

Figure 5-11. *Containers fresh screen under Monitor in Azure Portal*

Azure Kubernetes Service monitoring comes with variance implementation and unique requirements. This approach relies on these requirements. It deals with different layers, from infrastructure to application, and comes with distinct monitoring requirements based on the layer.

Considering a bottom-up approach, these layers can be listed as shown in Figure 5-12.

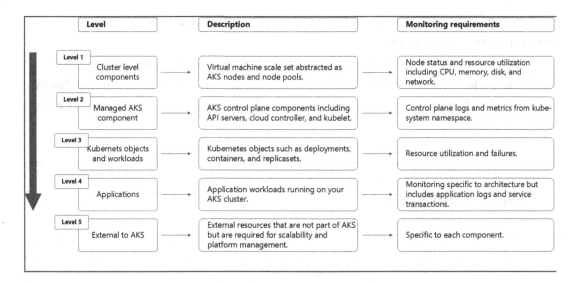

Level	Description	Monitoring requirements
Level 1 Cluster level components	Virtual machine scale set abstracted as AKS nodes and node pools.	Node status and resource utilization including CPU, memory, disk, and network.
Level 2 Managed AKS component	AKS control plane components including API servers, cloud controller, and kubelet.	Control plane logs and metrics from kube-system namespace.
Level 3 Kubernets objects and workloads	Kubernetes objects such as deployments, containers, and replicasets.	Resource utilization and failures.
Level 4 Applications	Application workloads running on your AKS cluster.	Monitoring specific to architecture but includes application logs and service transactions.
Level 5 External to AKS	External resources that are not part of AKS but are required for scalability and platform management.	Specific to each component.

Figure 5-12. *Layers of AKSImage source: Microsoft Documentation*

To maintain the scope and brevity of this chapter, I will discuss Level 4, the monitoring application layer that includes application workloads running in an AKS Cluster.

This layer mainly focuses on monitoring the microservices application and identifying application failures, along with information like request rates, response time, any exceptions encountered, and so on. For complete monitoring of applications running on AKS, you can use Application Insights, as shown in Figure 5-13.

Figure 5-13. *Icon for Application Insights*

Depending on your application stack, you need to configure code-based monitoring to collect the required data. It could be anything—Java, Python, .Net, or any other platform. In this example, I am more interested in ASP.NET Core applications.

You need to have a valid Application Insights instrumentation key and create the Application Insight resource.

To create one, go to Azure Subscription. Type **Application Insights** in the search and click Create New. You will be presented with the screen to add the basic mandatory details required to create the service. Enter with all the details and click Review + Create. Refer to Figure 5-14.

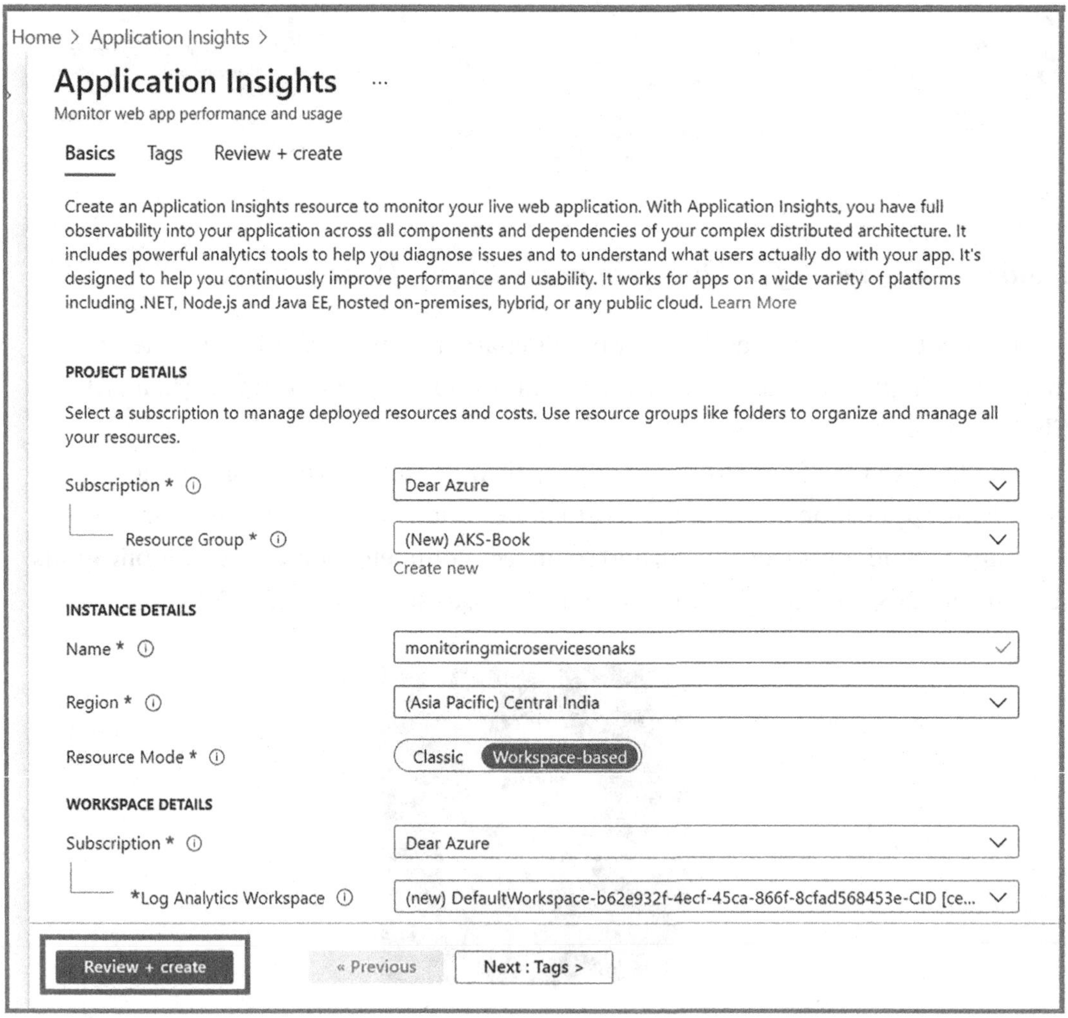

Figure 5-14. *Screen to create Application Insights in Azure Portal*

Once it's validated, click Create to complete the service creation.

Go to the newly created service screen to find the instrumentation key, connection string, and other details, all under the Overview section. Refer to the highlighted sections in Figure 5-15.

Figure 5-15. *Instrumentation keys for Application Insights in Azure Portal*

Tip   Using a connection string is highly recommended over an instrumentation key, as new Azure regions require connection strings. In either case, you need to create the service.

Next, you need enable Application Insights in your IDE. My favorite IDE is Visual Studio, but you can use other IDEs, such as like Visual Code, as well. Once you are done enabling Application Insights server-side telemetry with your IDE, download the latest stable release of the SDK by choosing NuGet Packages ➤ Microsoft.ApplicationInsights. AspNetCore. Refer to Figure 15-16.

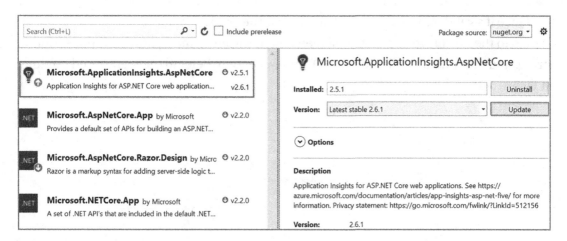

Figure 15-16. *SDK from the NuGet packageImage source: Microsoft Documentation*

By adding a few lines of code to the application, it will start with the telemetry data, and it can be presented in the Applications Insights screen in Azure Portal. This data can be analyzed and can be used to create alerts based on the state of your applications.

For the code and other options, refer to `https://docs.microsoft.com/en-us/azure/azure-monitor/app/asp-net-core`.

Summary

This chapter presented things you should know about securing and monitoring AKS-based applications. With the provided links, make sure you have proper hands-on experience with these issues. This chapter ends the theoretical part of the book. The next chapter uses a practical step-by-step approach to implementing CICD for Azure Kubernetes Service-based applications. Until then, happy Azure learning.

CHAPTER 6

CI/CD for AKS

Introduction

You are now in the last chapter of the book. By now, you have learned about the design considerations of microservices and Azure Kubernetes Services. You're nearly ready to monitor and secure an Azure Kubernetes service-based application. In this last and final chapter, you learn about an important aspect of application deliverables, Continuous Integration and Continuous Deployment, focusing on Azure Kubernetes Services-based applications.

A Quick Look at DevOps

I assume you are not new to this topic, but to start the chapter, I present a short introduction to DevOps.

DevOps brings together people, processes, and technology, automating software delivery to provide continuous value to your users. DevOps automates and speeds software delivery. It makes your process and your products more reliable.

DevOps is process, a practice, and a set of tools or a summation of all. It works together toward a quicker software/product deliverable adopted by an organization. It amplifies the team unification to a great extent, helping to make the development phase seamless. The main reason for its popularity is the faster deliverables. You code and add in a repository, and CI builds the application with the latest changes and presents it with a deployable artifact. This artifact is now taken and pushed live, and all this is part of the CD process flows. This can be done for all the environments you are working for. The same artifacts can be promoted to higher environments, such as from Development to QA to UAT to Production.

© Kasam Ahmed Shaikh and Shailesh S. Agaskar 2022
K. Ahmed Shaikh and S. S. Agaskar, *Azure Kubernetes Services with Microservices*,
https://doi.org/10.1007/978-1-4842-7809-3_6

Note   If you are a beginner to the DevOps concept, it's best to go through the documentation found at `https://docs.microsoft.com/en-us/learn/` `modules/get-started-with-devops/2-what-is-devops`.

To make this final chapter more interesting, I present the exercise in a step-by-step method. It has less theory and more practical applications. I am sure this will not only make your learning interesting, but will also help you understand the topic more easily. ☺

As a part of the prerequisites for the following exercise, you need to have a valid Microsoft Azure subscription, Visual Studio as the IDE, an Azure DevOps project, and Docker Desktop for Windows installed on your machine. The exercise uses GitHub as the source code repository.

Goals of This Exercise

Here is the agenda of this exercise:

- Create an Azure Kubernetes Service using Azure Portal.

- Create an Azure Container Instance using Azure Portal.

- Work with Visual Studio to build the sample application.

You can achieve CI/CD with various tools, but if you're a Microsoft Cloud enthusiast, the following tools are among the best:

- Azure DevOps

- GitHub Actions

The chapter presents you with the steps for using Azure DevOps. For GitHub Actions, you'll get a reference link, and you can try it as your first exercise in this chapter. Most of the detailed steps in this chapter are self-explanatory, but I include more details wherever it's required.

So get ready and follow these steps! ☺

Creating Azure Kubernetes Service Using Azure Portal

1. Open the Microsoft Azure Portal from `http://portal.azure.com/` and click the Create a Resource link, as shown in Figure 6-1.

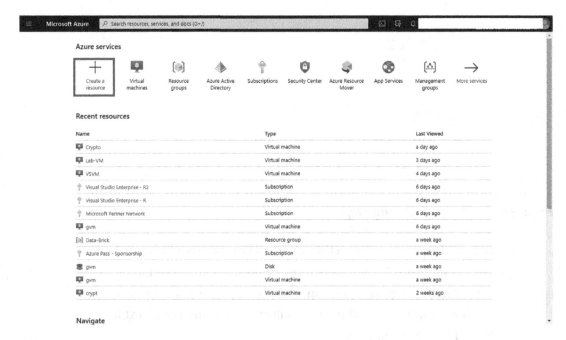

***Figure 6-1.** Image detailing Step 1*

2. Search for Kubernetes Service in the search box or navigate to Compute ➤ Kubernetes Service and click the service listed, as shown in Figure 6-2.

Figure 6-2. *Image detailing Step 2*

3. You will be presented with the screen to enter the basic details. Details such as selecting your subscription, resource group, cluster name, region, and so on. This example uses Kubernetes version 1.19.11. Enter all the mandatory details and click Next for Node Pools. See Figure 6-3.

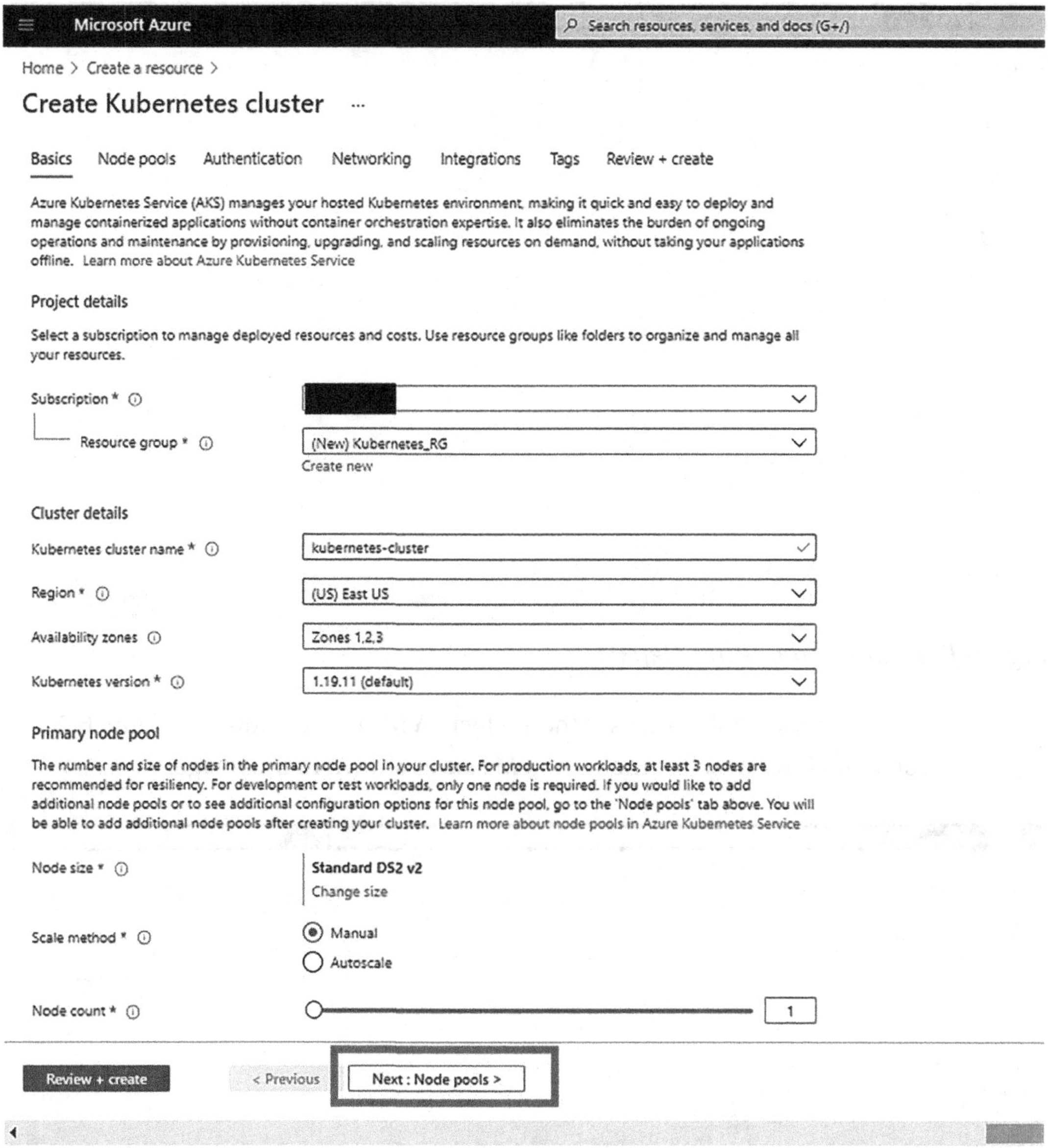

Figure 6-3. *Image detailing Step 3*

4. Now you'll add a node pool. Click the + Add Node Pool button.
    You are presented with multiple options, as shown in Figure 6-4.

Figure 6-4. *Image detailing Step 04*

5. Give the node pool name and then select a VM size, as shown in Figure 6-5.
   You don't have to select the same VM size as shown in the image.

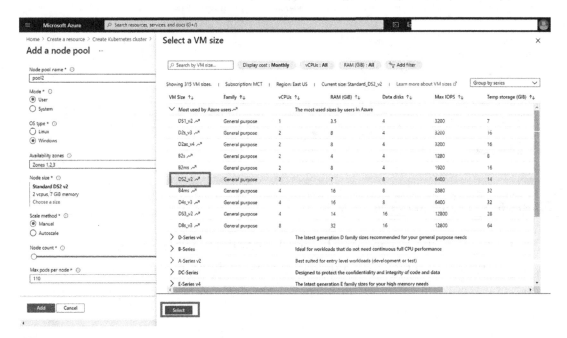

Figure 6-5. *Image detailing Step 5*

6. The newly created node will be listed. Click Next to move to Authentication. See Figure 6-6.

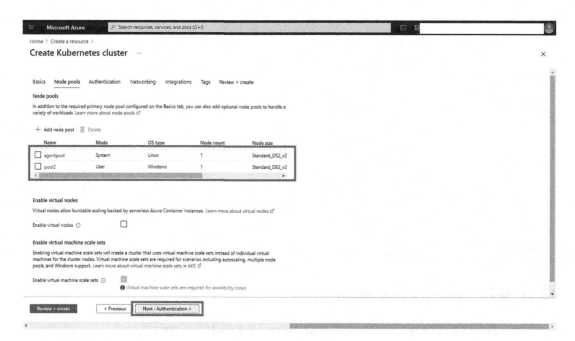

Figure 6-6. *Image detailing Step 6*

7. Select the authentication method and RBAC roles, as shown in Figure 6-7. Click Next.

Figure 6-7. *Image detailing Step 7*

8.   Select Network Configuration as Azure CNI and the other
mandatory fields, as shown in Figure 6-8.

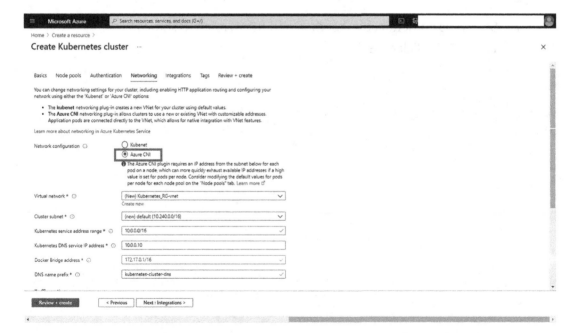

Figure 6-8. *Image detailing Step 8*

9. Make sure you select Azure for the network policy, as shown in Figure 6-9.

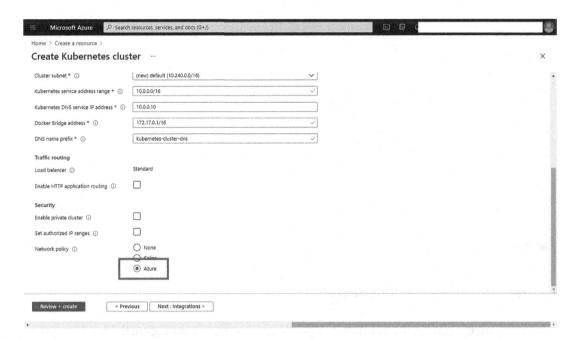

Figure 6-9. *Image detailing Step 9*

10. Click Next and present with the integration details. I will go as is. Click 'Review + Create, as shown in Figure 6-10.

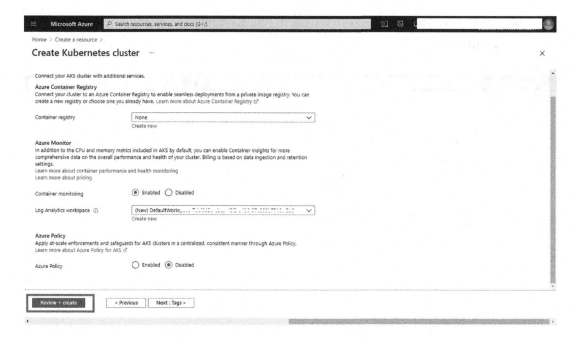

Figure 6-10. *Image detailing Step 10*

11.   Once it passes the validation, click Create, as shown in Figure 6-11.

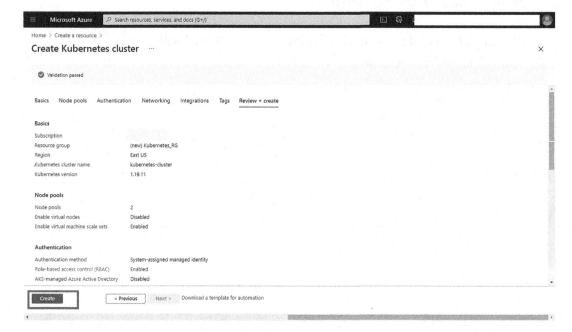

Figure 6-11. *Image detailing Step 11*

12. This will lead to the screen presenting the progress of deployment. Click Go to Resource upon successful completion of deployment, as shown in Figure 6-12.

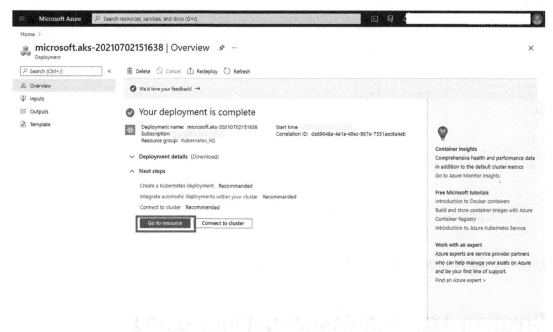

Figure 6-12. *Image detailing Step 12*

13. You will be presented with the newly created Kubernetes Cluster, as shown in Figure 6-13.

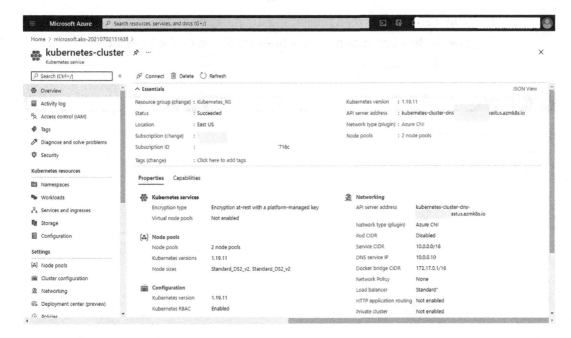

Figure 6-13. *Image detailing Step 13*

Creating Azure Container Instance Using Azure Portal

14.   Follow the step shown in Figure 6-14.

Figure 6-14. *Image detailing Step 14*

15.   Follow the step shown in Figure 6-15.

Figure 6-15. *Image detailing Step 15*

16. Enter the mandatory details on the Basic screen and leave the rest set to the defaults. Click Review + Create, as shown in Figure 6-16.

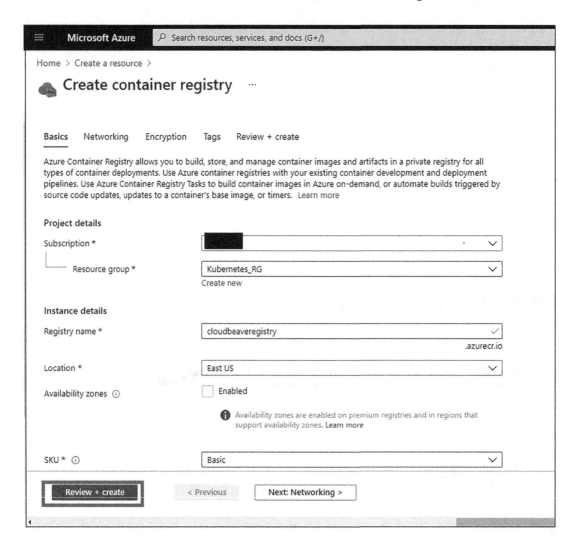

Figure 6-16. *Image detailing Step 16*

17. Once you see that validation has passed, click Create. See Figure 6-17.

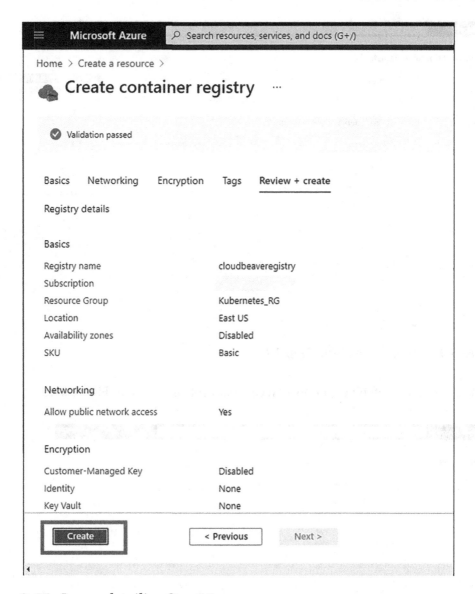

Figure 6-17. *Image detailing Step 17*

18. Wait for the deployment to complete. Click Go to Resource, as
     shown in Figure 6-18.

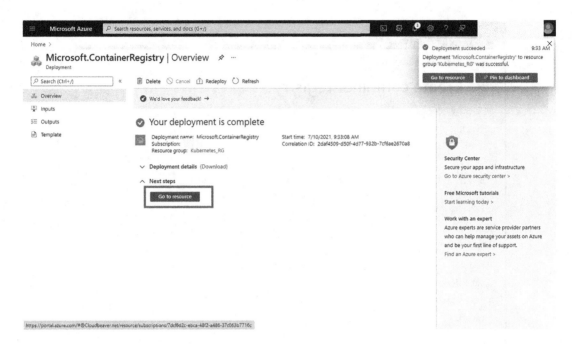

Figure 6-18. *Image detailing Step 18*

19.   From the left blade, choose Access Control, as shown in Figure 6-19.

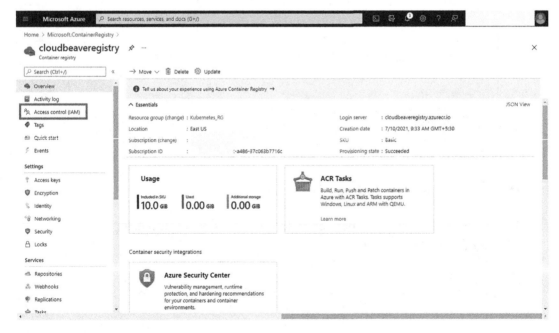

Figure 6-19. *Image detailing Step 19*

20.   Click to add a new role assignment, as shown in Figure 6-20.

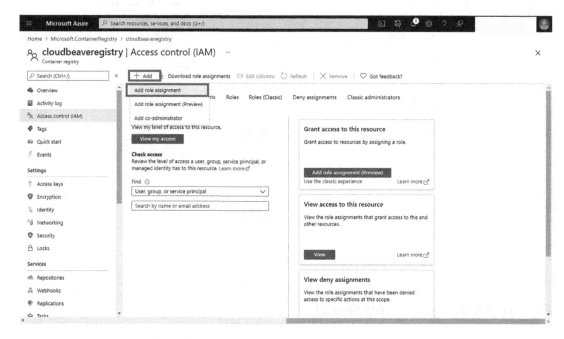

Figure 6-20.   *Image detailing Step 20*

21.   Select the ÁrcPull role that presents user managed identity and
then select the newly created pool, as shown in Figure 6-21.

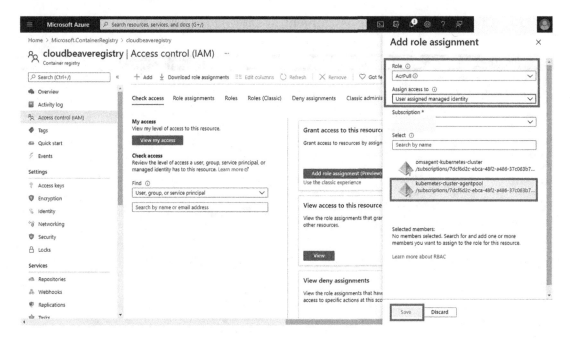

Figure 6-21. *Image detailing Step 21*

22.   Follow the step shown in Figure 6-22.

Figure 6-22. *Image detailing Step 22*

23.   From the left blade, go to Access Keys under the Settings section, as shown in Figure 6-23.

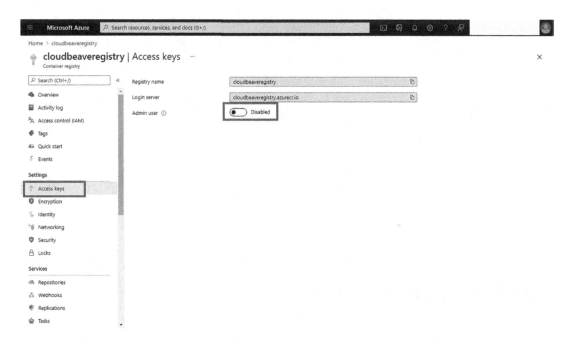

Figure 6-23. *Image detailing Step 23*

24.   Click Toggle to enable the keys as the Admin User, as shown in Figure 6-24.

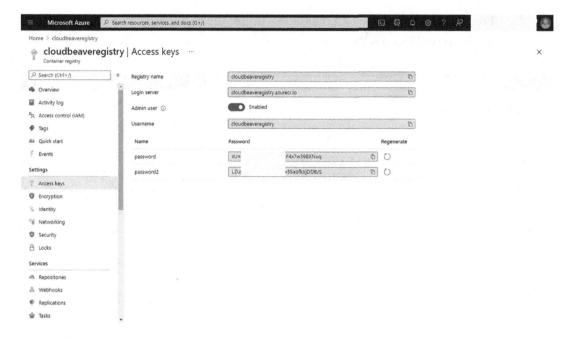

Figure 6-24. *Image detailing Step 24*

Working with Visual Studio to Build the Sample Application

25. Before opening up the IDE, go to the following link to download the Docker Desktop and install it with the default settings: https://www.docker.com/products/docker-desktop (see Figure 6-25).

Figure 6-25. *Image detailing Step 25*

26.   Figure 6-26 shows that Docker is up and running.

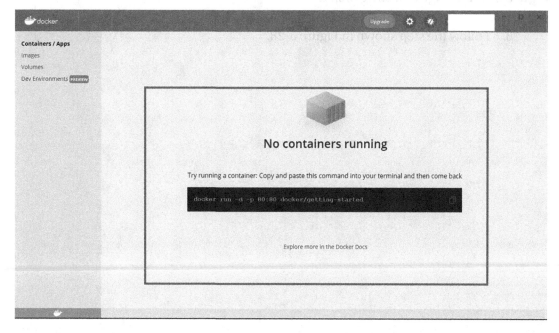

Figure 6-26. *Image detailing Step 26*

27. Now open Visual Studio and choose Create a New Project, as shown in Figure 6-27.

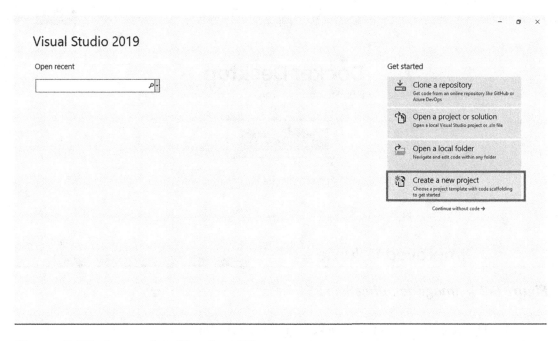

Figure 6-27. *Image detailing Step 27*

28. Follow the step shown in Figure 6-28.

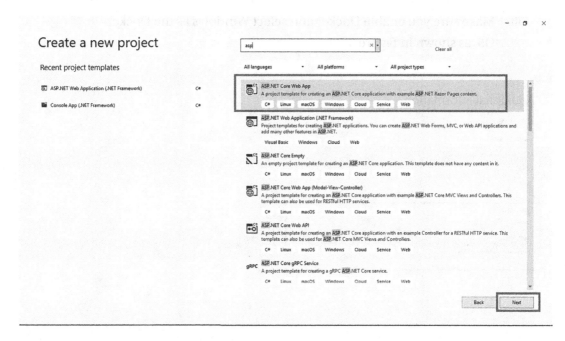

Figure 6-28. *Image detailing Step 28*

29.   Choose a name for the application, as shown in Figure 6-29.

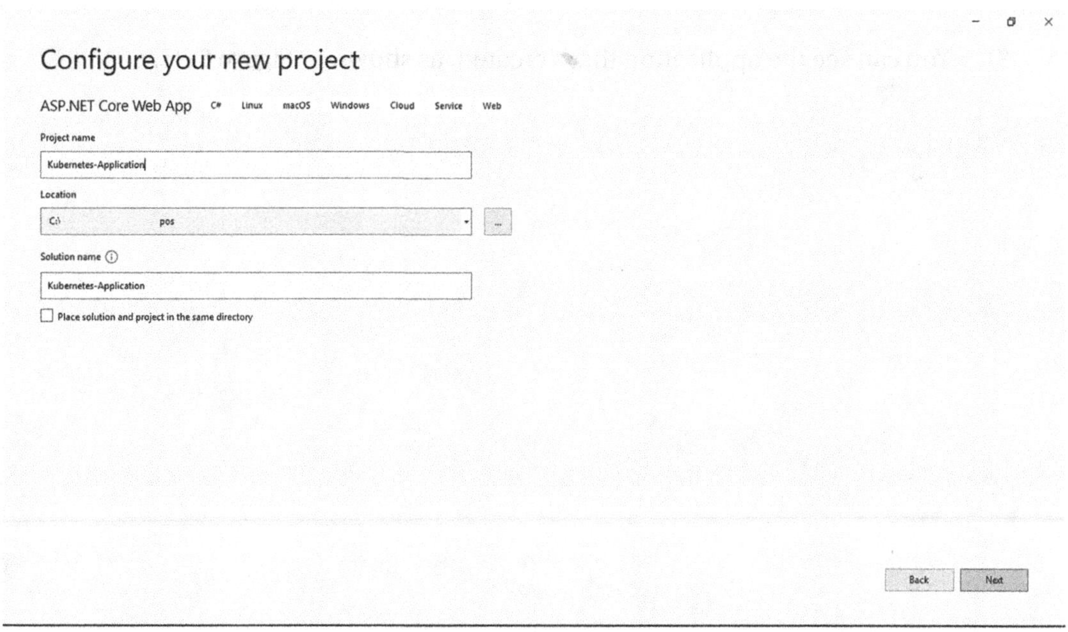

Figure 6-29. *Image detailing Step 29*

30. Make sure you enable Docker and select Windows as the Docker OS, as shown in Figure 6-30.

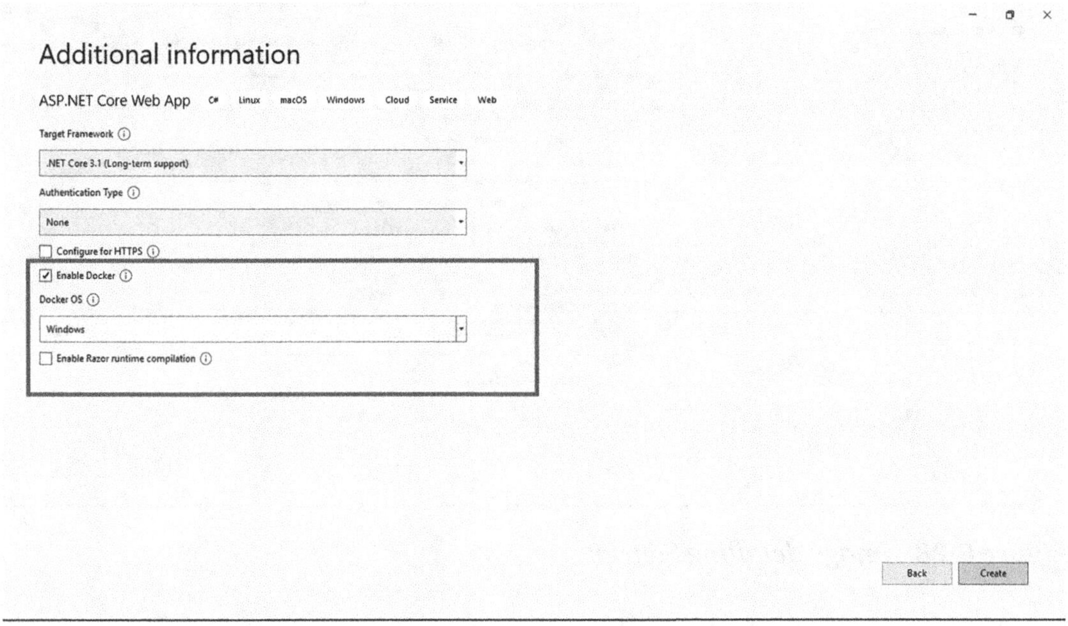

Figure 6-30. *Image detailing Step 30*

31. You can see the application that's created, as shown in Figure 6-31.

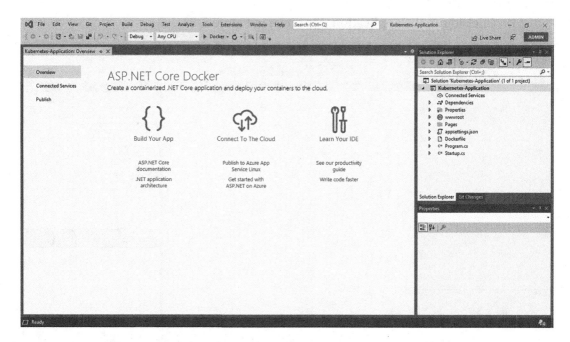

Figure 6-31. *Image detailing Step 31*

32.   Select Run ➤ Kubernetes Application , as shown in Figure 6-32.

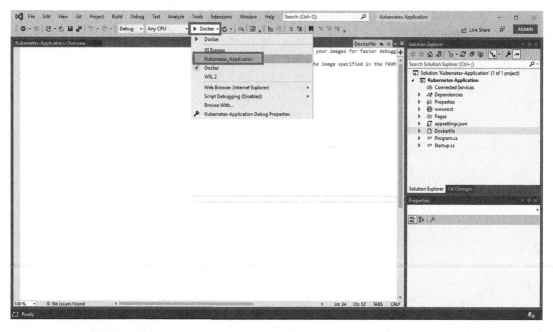

Figure 6-32. *Image detailing Step 32*

33.   Click to run the application, as shown in Figure 6-33.

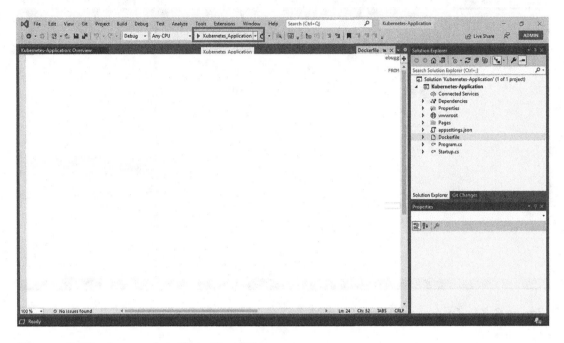

Figure 6-33.   *Image detailing Step 33*

34.   Make sure the application is running fine, with no errors.
See Figure 6-34.

Figure 6-34. *Image detailing Step 34*

35.   Now add a new file by right-clicking and choosing Add ➤ New
        File. See Figure 6-35.

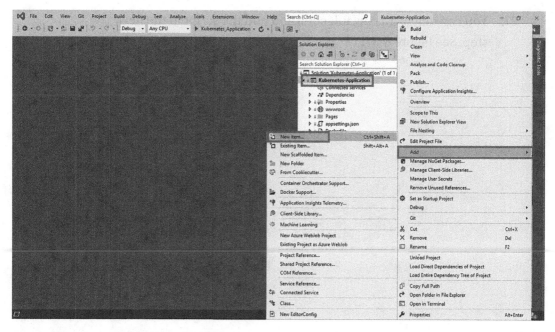

Figure 6-35. *Image detailing Step 35*

36.   You have to add this YAML file, as it defines the deployment
       details of your containers in Kubernetes. See Figure 6-36.

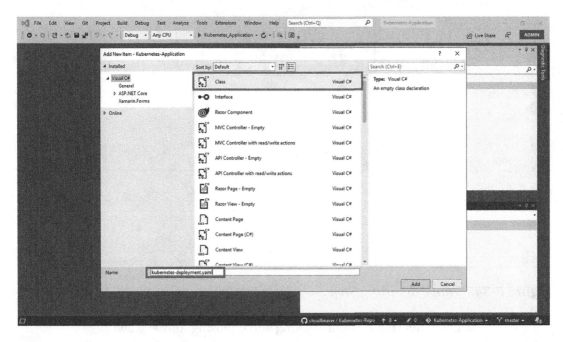

Figure 6-36. *Image detailing Step 36*

37.   You can delete this default code and add the script in the next
       step. See Figure 6-37.

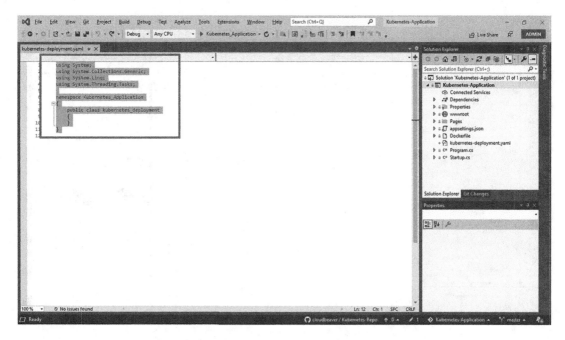

Figure 6-37. *Image detailing Step 37*

38.   The following script defines the details of container image, the
      number of copies it must create, the ports to be exposed, the
      scaling metrics, and the update policies. See Figure 6-38.

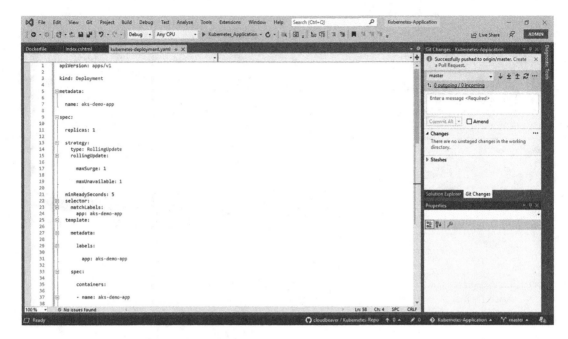

Figure 6-38. *Image detailing Step 38*

39. Follow the step shown in Figure 6-39.

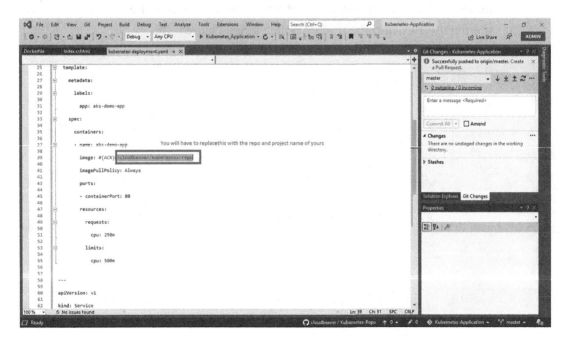

Figure 6-39. *Image detailing Step 39*

40. This complete script is helping to build a container application. This is default script, and you can change it according to your needs. See Figure 6-40.

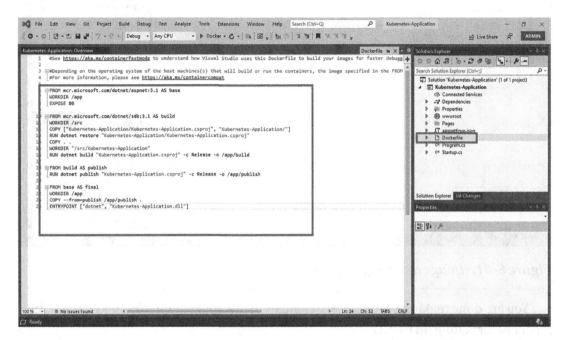

Figure 6-40. *Image detailing Step 40*

41. Replace the default script with the script in Figure 6-41. This script is taking the dotnet core container image as its base and building the container application.

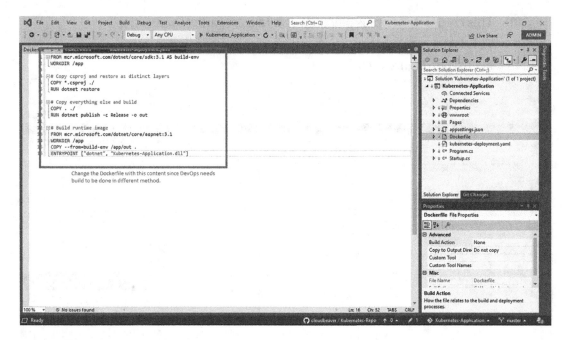

Figure 6-41. *Image detailing Step 41*

You are done making the necessary changes in the application. Now you'll build the pipelines for setting up CI/CD.

CI/CD with Azure DevOps

42.   Open the Team Explorer and follow the step shown in Figure 6-42.

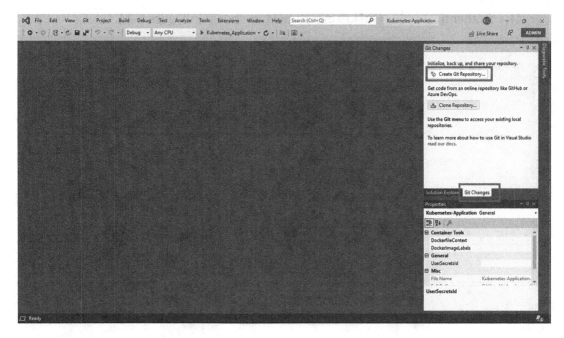

Figure 6-42. *Image detailing Step 42*

43. Connect to the GitHub repository by following the step shown in Figure 6-43.

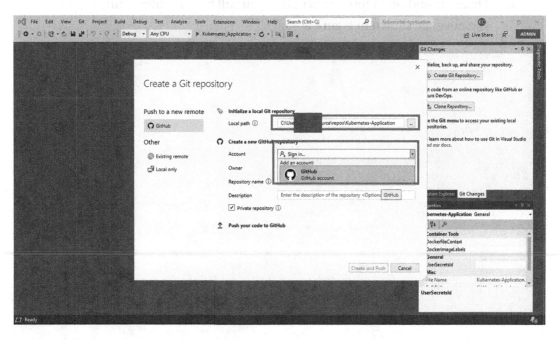

Figure 6-43. *Image detailing Step 43*

44. Authenticate your GitHub credentials, as shown in Figure 6-44.

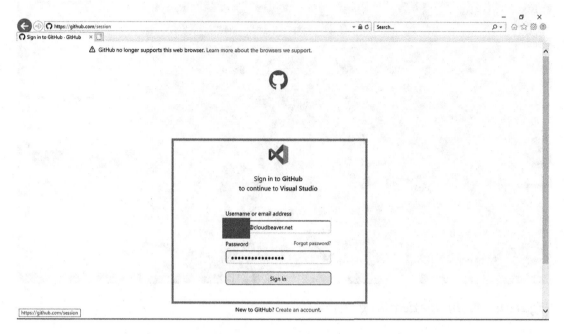

Figure 6-44. *Image detailing Step 44*

45. Once the authorization is successful, you will be presented with
     the message shown in Figure 6-45.

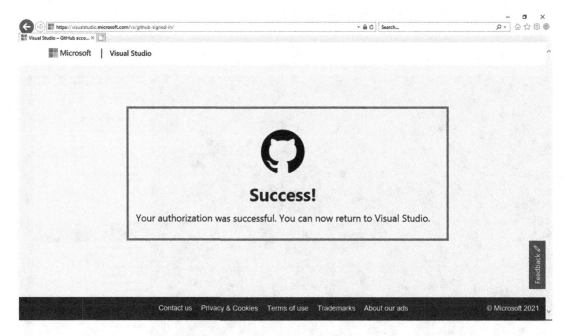

Figure 6-45. *Image detailing Step 45*

46.   Follow the step shown in Figure 6-46.

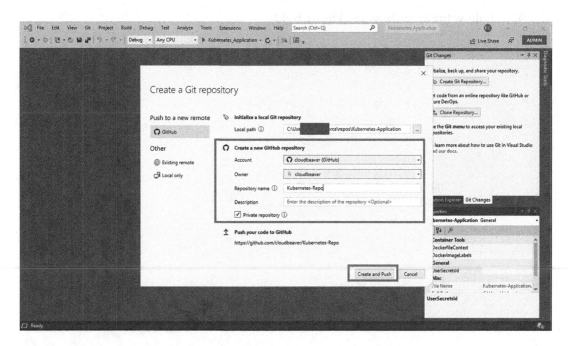

Figure 6-46. *Image detailing Step 46*

47.   Follow the step shown in Figure 6-47.

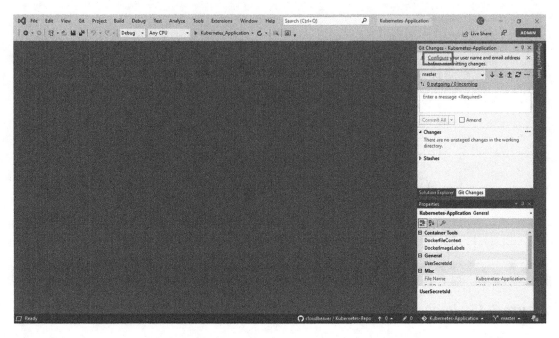

Figure 6-47. *Image detailing Step 47*

48.   Follow the step shown in Figure 6-48.

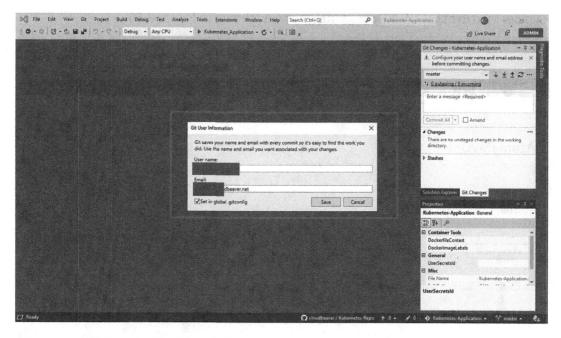

Figure 6-48. *Image detailing Step 48*

49.   The application you created is now part of your repo, and files can be seen, as shown in Figure 6-49.

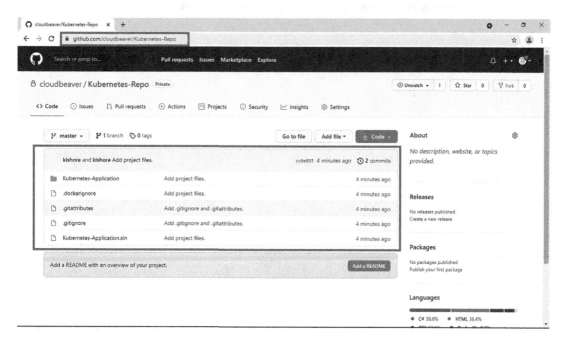

Figure 6-49. *Image detailing Step 49*

50.   Go to https://devops.azure.com/, as shown in Figure 6-50.

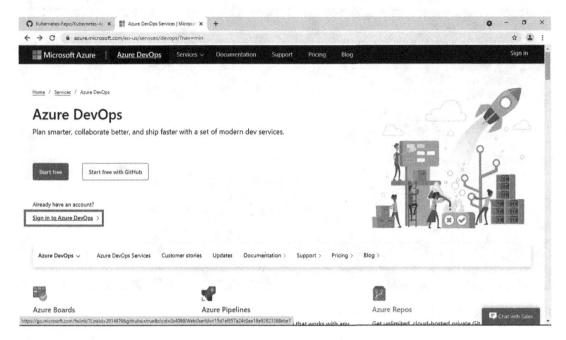

Figure 6-50. *Image detailing Step 50*

51.   Follow the step shown in Figure 6-51 to create a new project.

Figure 6-51. *Image detailing Step 51*

52.   Follow the step shown in Figure 6-52.

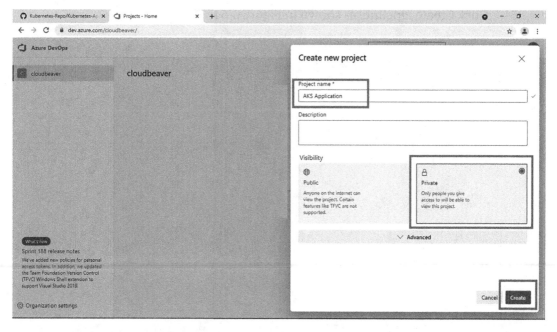

Figure 6-52. *Image detailing Step 52*

53.   To start the Pipelines, follow the step shown in Figure 6-53.

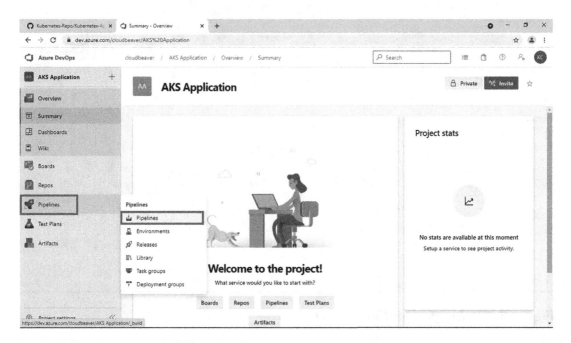

Figure 6-53. *Image detailing Step 53*

54.   Click Create Pipeline, as shown in Figure 6-54.

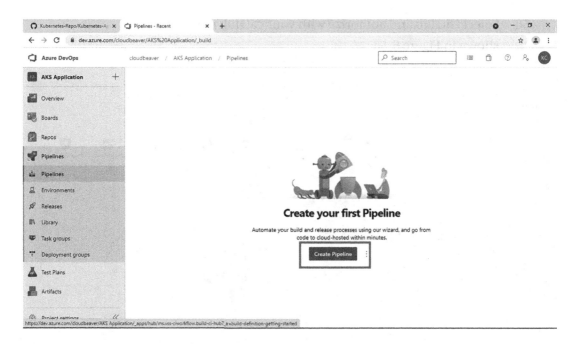

Figure 6-54. *Image detailing Step 54*

55.   Pick your code; this example uses the Classic Editor, as shown in
Figure 6-55.

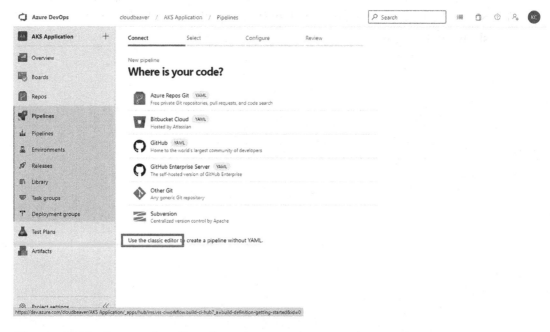

Figure 6-55. *Image detailing Step 55*

56.   Select GitHub and authorize with your GitHub credentials, as
shown in Figure 6-56.

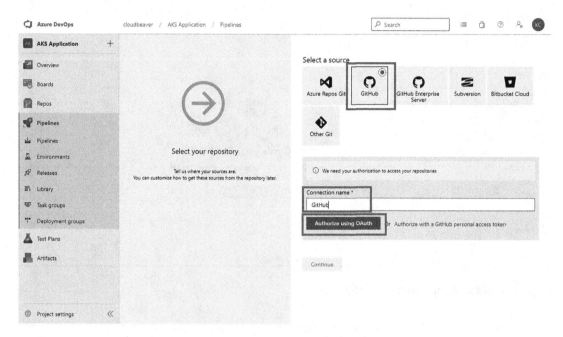

Figure 6-56. *Image detailing Step 56*

57.   Select the Repository where you have your application files, as
shown in Figure 6-57.

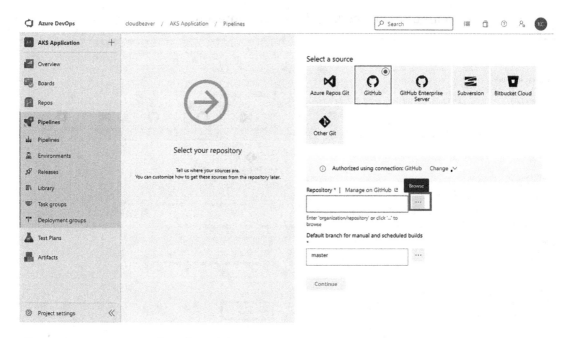

Figure 6-57. *Image detailing Step 57*

58. Follow the step shown in Figure 6-58.

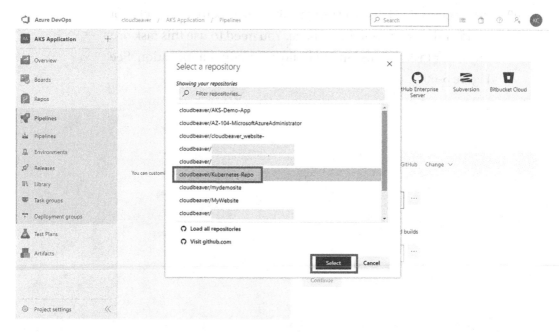

Figure 6-58. *Image detailing Step 58*

59.   Click Continue to proceed, as shown in Figure 6-59.

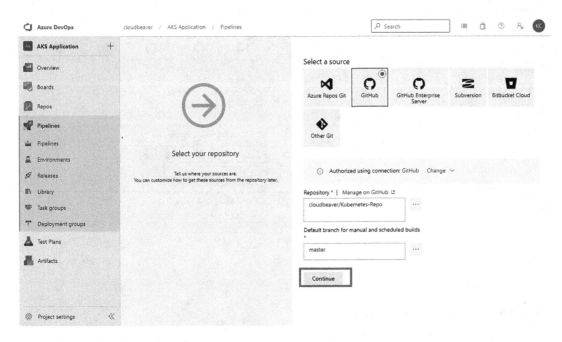

Figure 6-59. *Image detailing Step 59*

60.   Add a new task. This is a DevOps pipeline task that can help you
build and push a container image. You need to use this task or
any other tasks of this kind to build a container application. See
Figure 6-60.

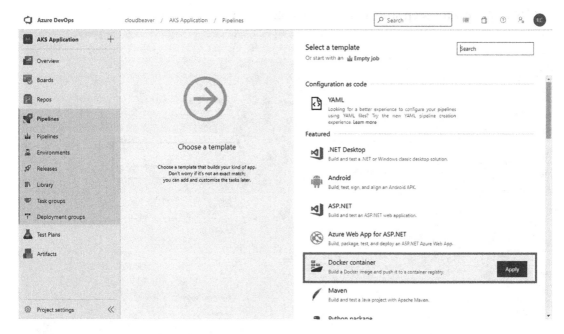

Figure 6-60. *Image detailing Step 60*

61.   Follow the step shown in Figure 6-61.

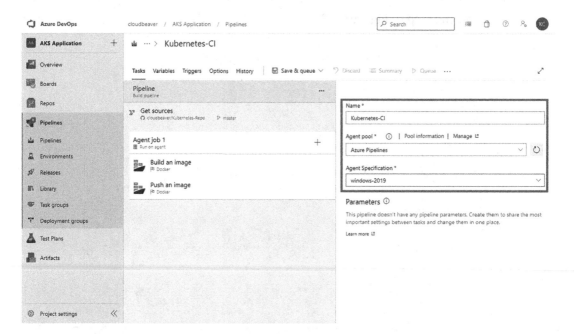

Figure 6-61. *Image detailing Step 61*

62.   Follow the step shown in Figure 6-62.

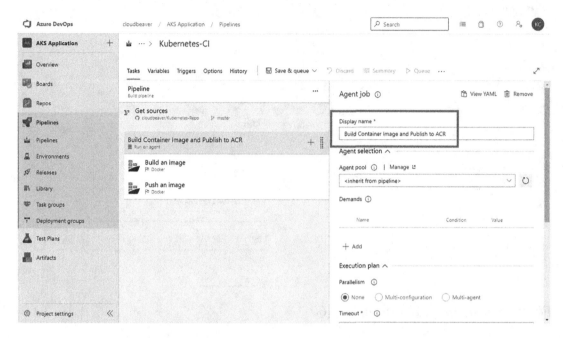

Figure 6-62.   *Image detailing Step 62*

63.   Follow the step in Figure 6-63.

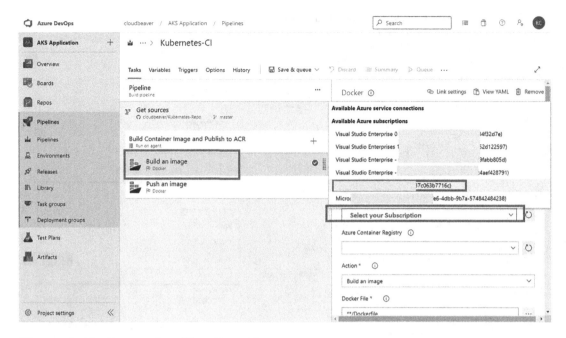

Figure 6-63. *Image detailing Step 63*

64. Authorize your subscription, as shown in Figure 6-64.

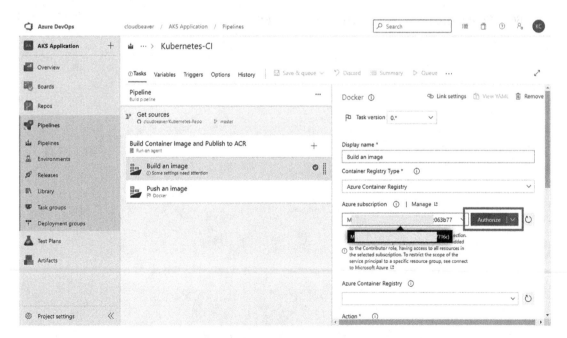

Figure 6-64. *Image detailing Step 64*

65.   Follow the step shown in Figure 6-65.

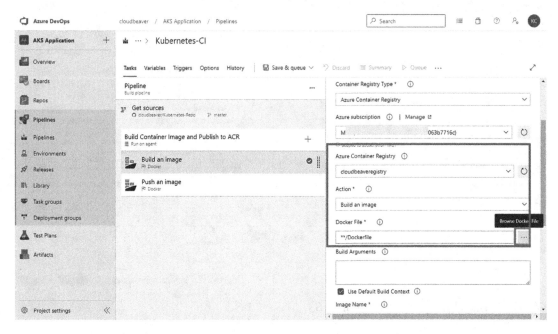

Figure 6-65. *Image detailing Step 65*

66.   Select the path, as shown in Figure 6-66.

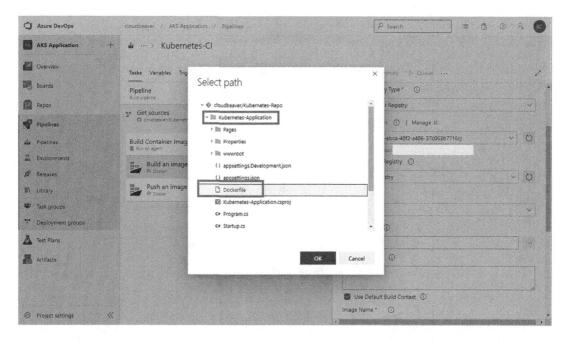

Figure 6-66. *Image detailing Step 66*

67. It is best to create a new version of the container for each build, as every new change in the code builds a container. Therefore, to keep the version of the image unique, use the build ID of the pipeline, which gets uniquely generated each time the pipeline runs build operations. The value shown in Figure 6-67 with the $ in front of it is a variable that comes in the DevOps pipeline.

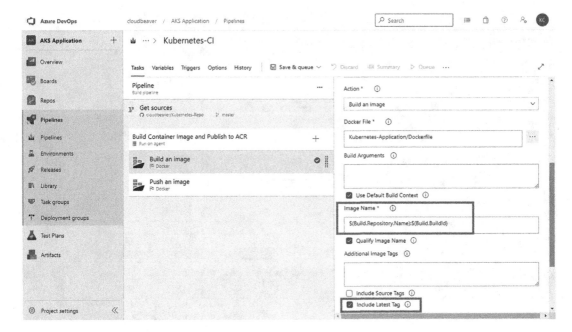

Figure 6-67. *Image detailing Step 67*

68.   Follow the step shown in Figure 6-68.

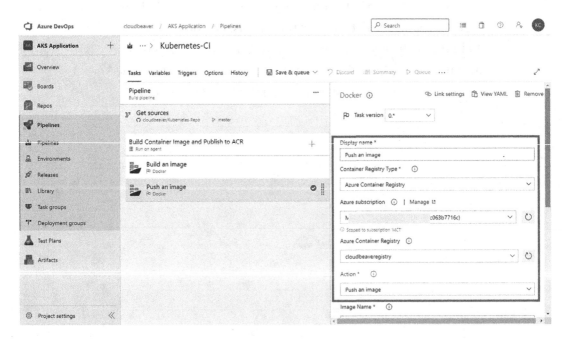

Figure 6-68. *Image detailing Step 68*

69. This is same as was mentioned for the previous build task of the Docker image. You need to provide a unique version for the Docker image that you are going to push into the ACR. Therefore, use the variable shown in Figure 6-69.

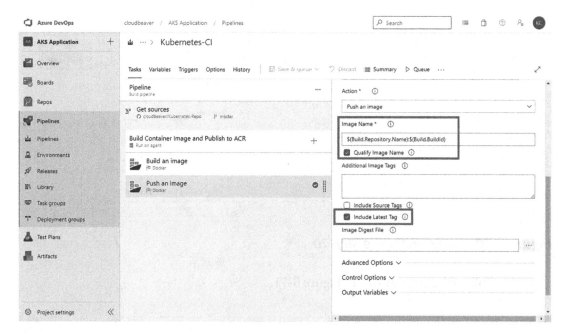

Figure 6-69. *Image detailing Step 69*

70. We can use the Replace Tokens task to replace the URL of the Azure Container Registry, which will be used to store a container image. Rather than hard-coding the URL of the registry in the source code, you create a variable in the YAML file that was initially added to define the container configuration for deployment into Kubernetes. Each time it runs, you can provide a variable in the pipeline so that during the pipeline's runtime, you can define the container registry details. See Figure 6-70.

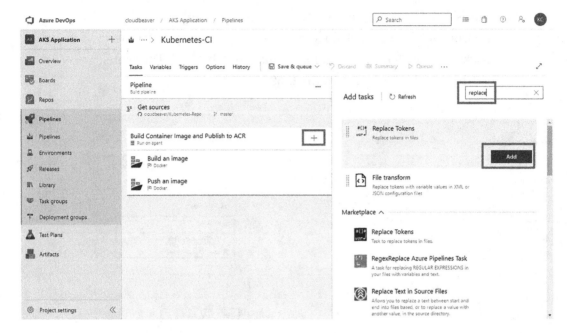

Figure 6-70. *Image detailing Step 70*

71.   Follow the step shown in Figure 6-71.

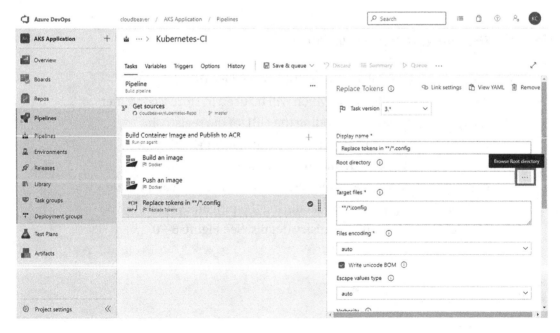

Figure 6-71. *Image detailing Step 71*

72.   Select the path, as shown in Figure 6-72.

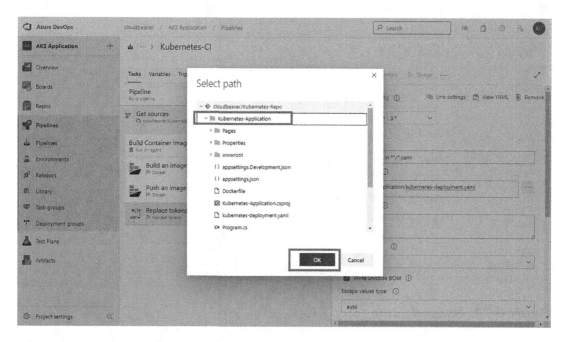

Figure 6-72. *Image detailing Step 72*

73.   Here you list the details of the file in which you want to replace the variable, which is the container registry name. See Figure 6-73.

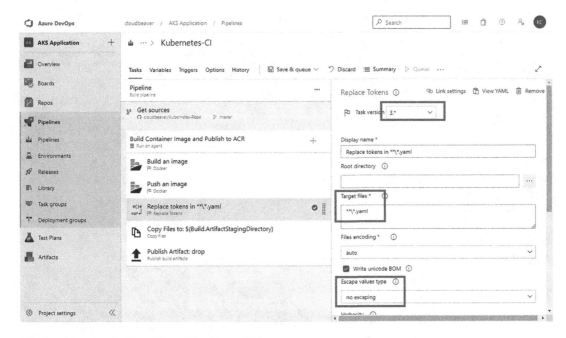

Figure 6-73. *Image detailing Step 73*

74.   Go to Variables and click the Add button, as shown in Figure 6-74.

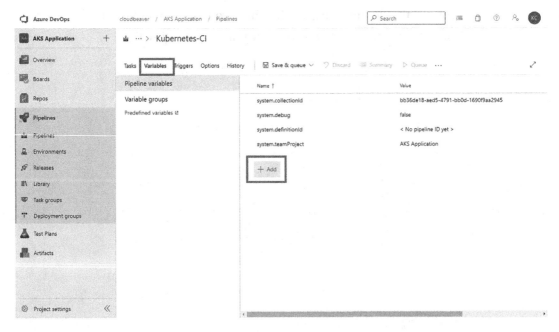

Figure 6-74. *Image detailing Step 74*

75.   Add ÁCR as a new variable name and the ACR login server URL
from the Azure Portal as the Value, as shown in Figure 6-75.

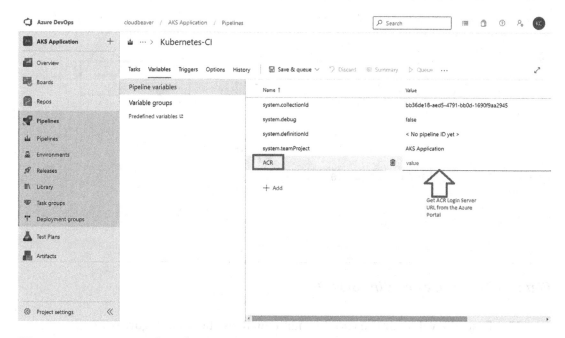

Figure 6-75. *Image detailing Step 75*

76.   In Azure Portal, get the required URL, as shown in Figure 6-76.

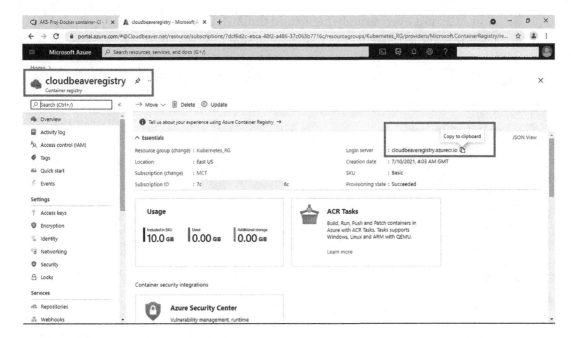

Figure 6-76. *Image detailing Step 76*

77. Paste the value for the variable name ACR, as shown in Figure 6-77.

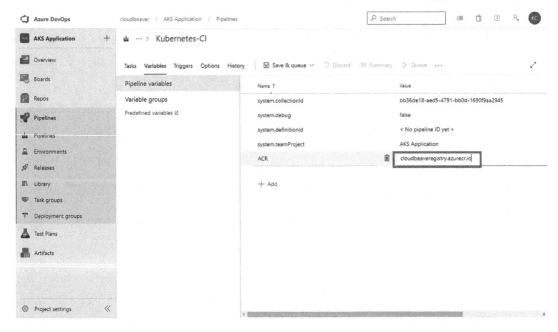

Figure 6-77. *Image detailing Step 77*

78.   Add new task name called Copy Files. Follow the step shown in Figure 6-78.

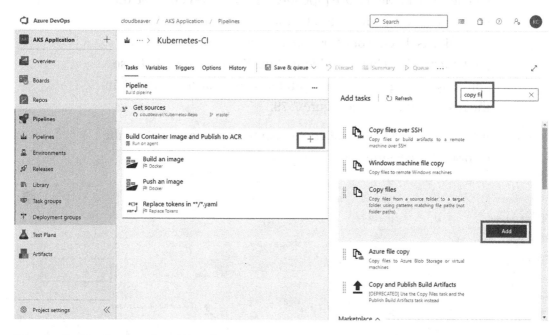

Figure 6-78. *Image detailing Step 78*

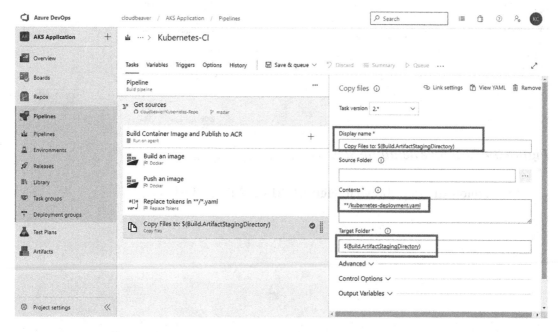

Figure 6-79. *Image detailing Step 79*

79. This is a build pipeline that builds your code and the built artifacts will be given to the release pipeline to release the code. Use the Copy File task to copy the built artifacts. But here, you don't have any artifacts that are built, as you are sending the image to the container registry in the build pipeline. You need the YAML, so you copy it using this task and publish it as an artifact to use it in the release pipeline. See Figure 7-79.

80. Add another task name called Publish Build Artifacts. Follow the step shown in Figure 6-80.

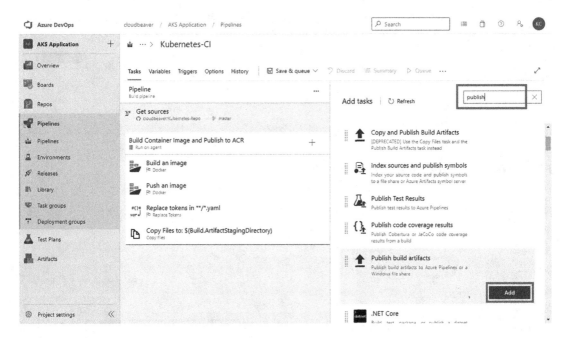

Figure 6-80. *Image detailing Step 80*

81. Follow the step shown in Figure 6-81 for Publish Task.

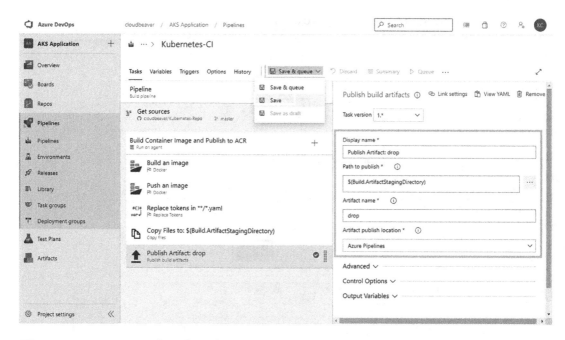

Figure 6-81. *Image detailing Step 81*

82. Go to the Triggers section and enable continuous integration by checking the option, as shown in Figure 6-82.

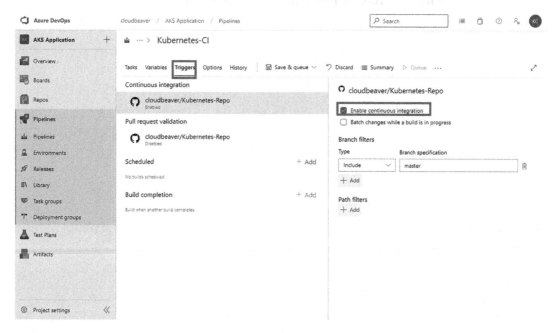

Figure 6-82. *Image detailing Step 82*

83.   Follow the step shown in Figure 6-83.

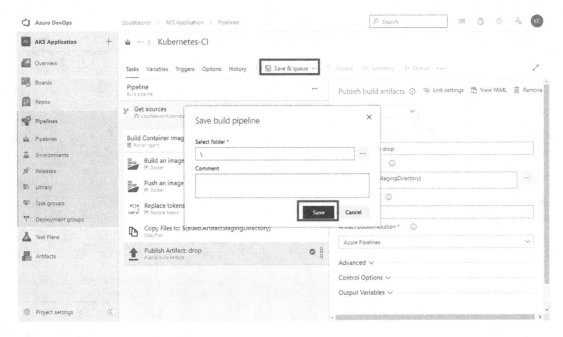

Figure 6-83. *Image detailing Step 83*

84.   Now you'll create release pipelines, as shown in Figure 6-84.

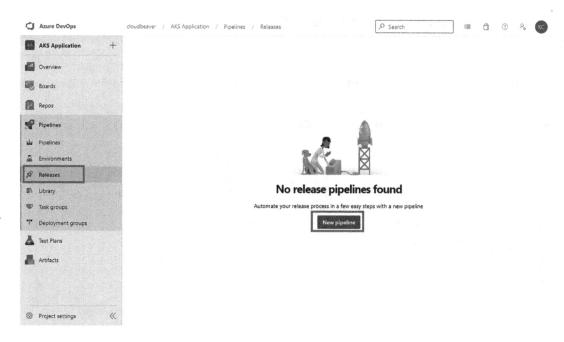

Figure 6-84. *Image detailing Step 84*

85.   Deploy to a Kubernetes Cluster task, as shown in Figure 6-85.

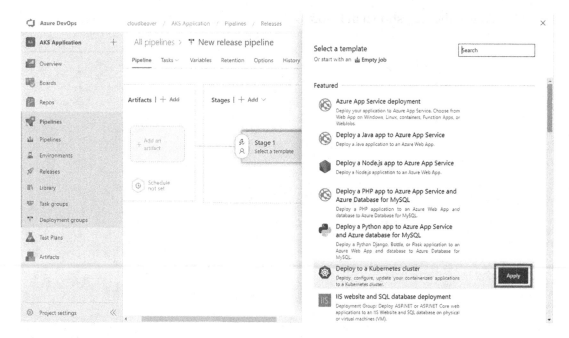

Figure 6-85. *Image detailing Step 85*

86. Give it a name, as shown in Figure 6-86.

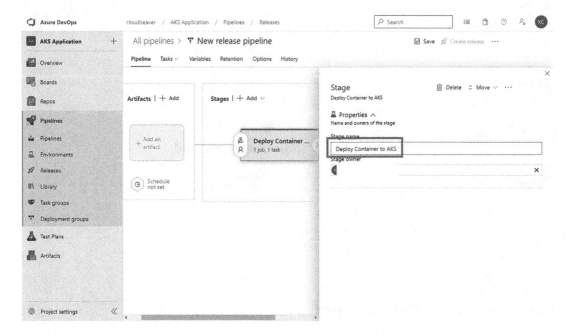

Figure 6-86. *Image detailing Step 86*

87. Follow the step shown in Figure 6-87.

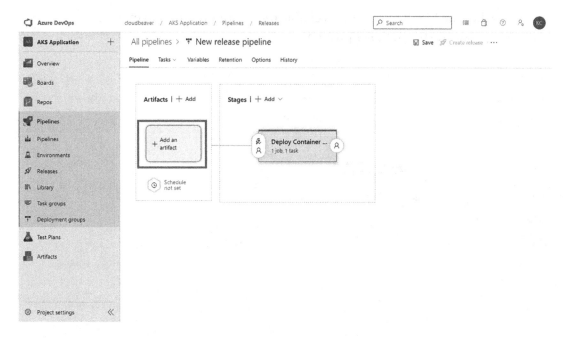

Figure 6-87. *Image detailing Step 87*

88.   Select the build and present it with the build pipeline you created
in the preceding steps as the source. See Figure 6-88.

Figure 6-88. *Image detailing Step 88*

89. Click the highlighted icon to enable the continuous deployment trigger, as shown in Figure 6-89.

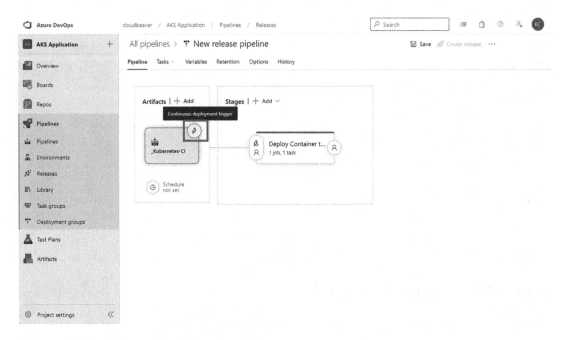

Figure 6-89. *Image detailing Step 89*

90. Enable it using the toggle, as shown in Figure 6-90.

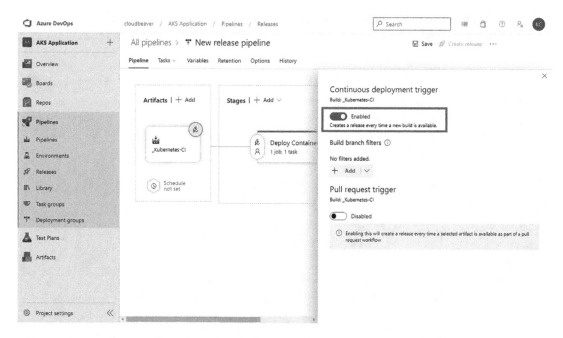

Figure 6-90. *Image detailing Step 90*

91.   Under Stage, click the Task link to proceed. See Figure 6-91.

Figure 6-91. *Image detailing Step 91*

92. Against the task, click New to create a new service connection. See
     Figure 6-92.

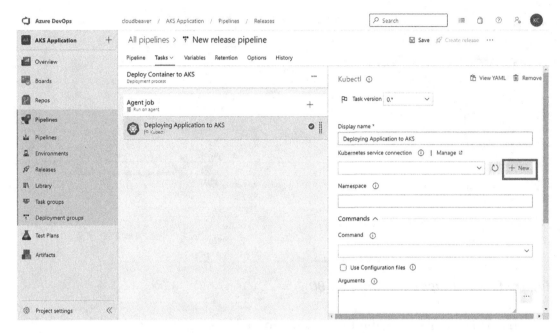

Figure 6-92. *Image detailing Step 92*

93. Select Azure Subscription as the Authentication method and
     select the subscription, resource group, and namespace as the
     defaults. Enter a name for the service connection and click Save.
     See Figure 6-93.

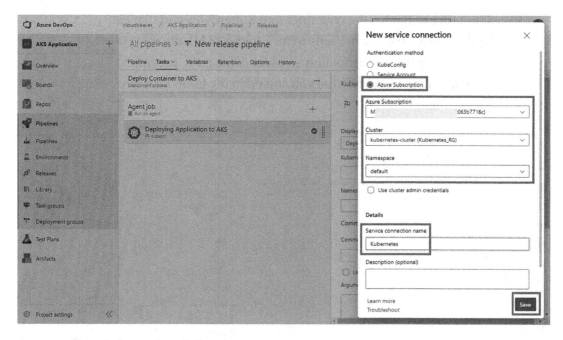

Figure 6-93. *Image detailing Step 93*

94.   Proceed with the details, as shown in Figure 6-94.

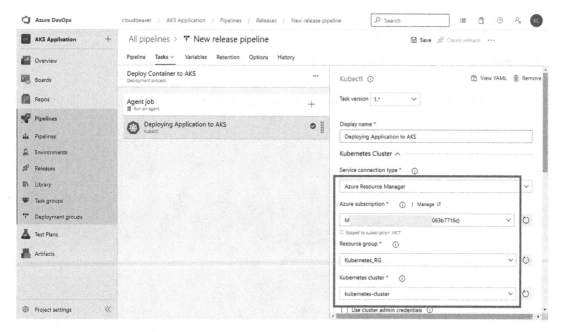

Figure 6-94. *Image detailing Step 94*

95. This task will deploy the container into Kubernetes and that can be done using the instructions written in the YAML file that you published in the build pipeline. In place of file path, provide the path of the YAML file that you copied in the build task. See Figure 6-95.

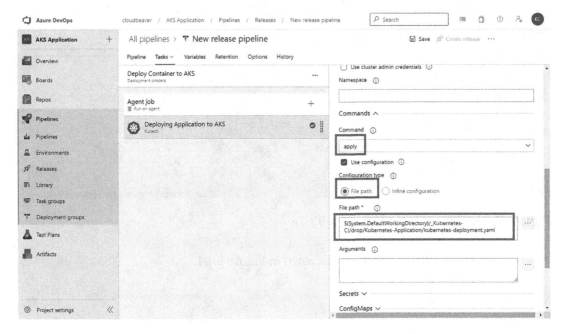

Figure 6-95. *Image detailing Step 95*

96. Enter the Secrets details, as shown in Figure 6-96.

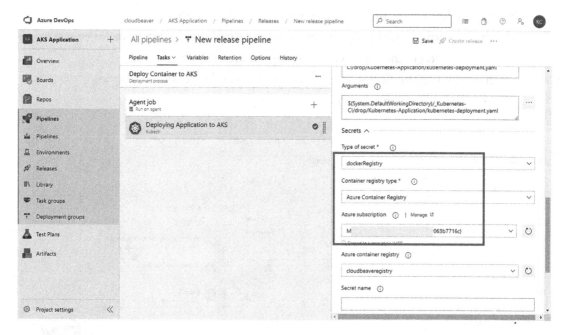

Figure 6-96. *Image detailing Step 96*

97.   Select the latest version to make sure that the deployment works fine. See Figure 6-97.

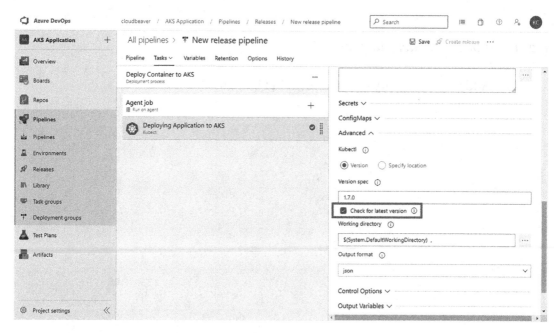

Figure 6-97. *Image detailing Step 97*

98.   When deploying the next version of the container application into the Kubernetes by changing the source code of the application, you should get the latest container application. To make that happen, use the Kubectl set command to set the version of the container; see Figure 6-98.

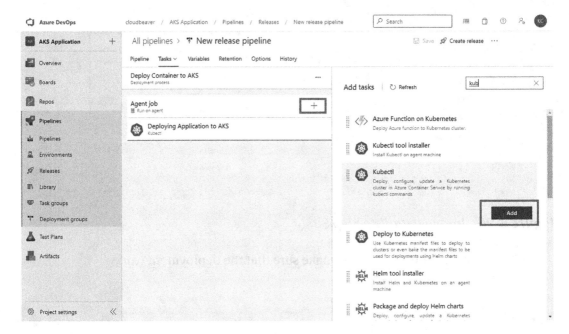

Figure 6-98.   *Image detailing Step 98*

99.   Add the mandatory details shown in Figure 6-99.

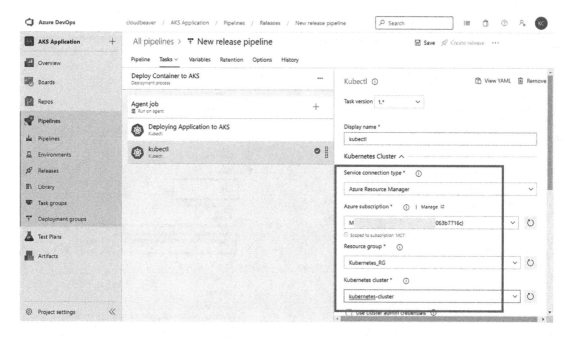

Figure 6-99. *Image detailing Step 99*

100. Since each build creates a new version of the container, use the
      build ID variable with the Kubectl set command to set the same
      version of the image that was built as the latest version of image to
      be deployed in the Kubernetes. See Figure 6-100.

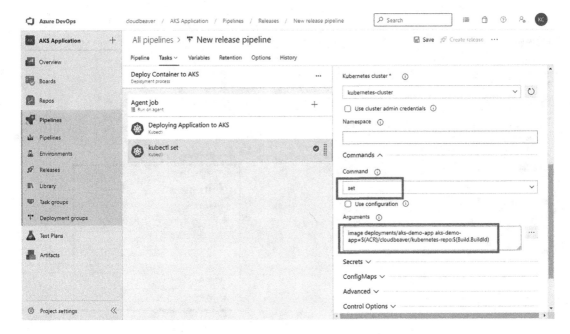

Figure 6-100. *Image detailing Step 100*

101.   Go to the Variables section and add variable name called
        ACR. Use the same ACR server DNS. See Figure 6-101.

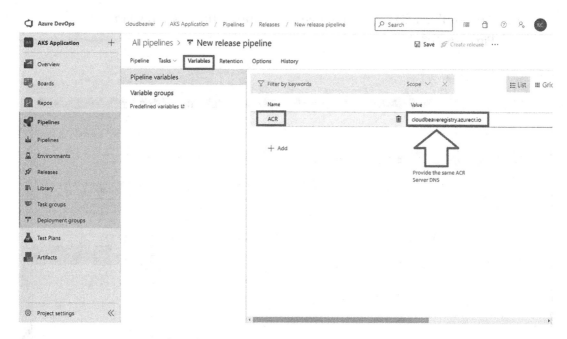

Figure 6-101. *Image detailing Step 101*

102.   Follow the step shown in Figure 6-102.

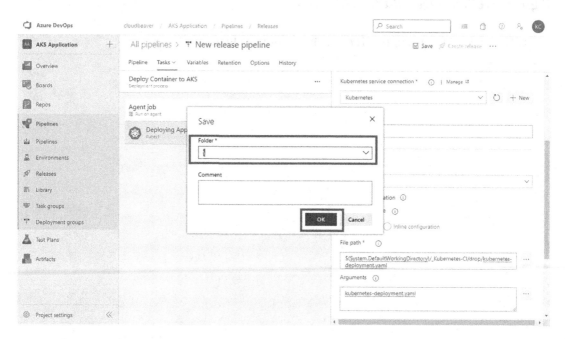

Figure 6-102. *Image detailing Step 102*

103.   Now you'll make a small change to the application, as shown in
        Figure 6-103.

Figure 6-103. *Image detailing Step 103*

104.   Make changes to the Index.chtml file; see Figure 6-104.

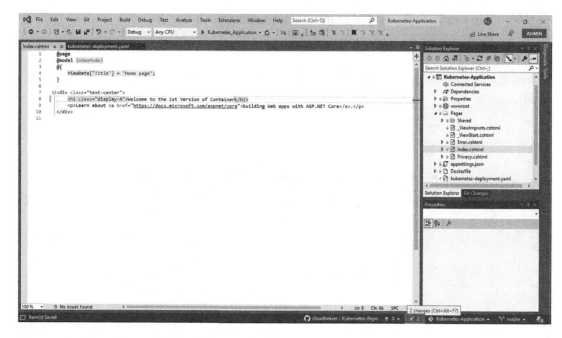

Figure 6-104. *Image detailing Step 104*

105.   Add the relevant comments and then commit and push the
        changes, as shown in Figure 6-105.

Figure 6-105. *Image detailing Step 105*

106.   You can view the added comment and changes under the
Pipelines section, as shown in Figure 6-106.

Figure 6-106. *Image detailing Step 106*

107.   Verify the changes. See Figure 6-107.

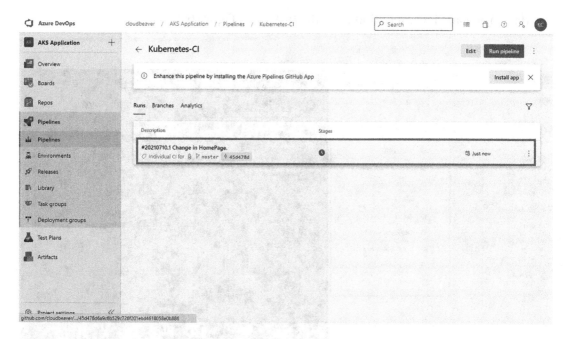

Figure 6-107. *Image detailing Step 107*

108.   Click and check the status. See Figure 6-108.

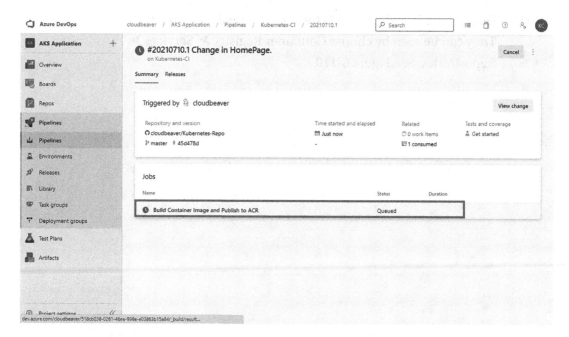

Figure 6-108. *Image detailing Step 108*

109.   You can view execution of all the tasks; see Figure 6-109.

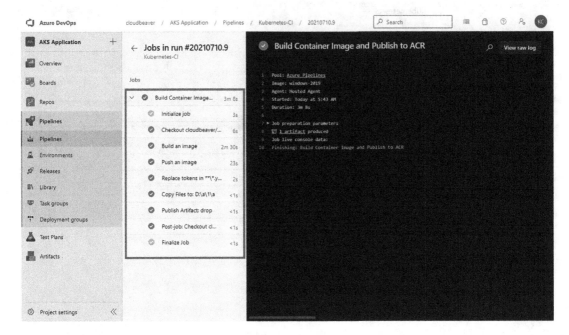

Figure 6-109. *Image detailing Step 109*

110.   Go to Azure Portal and verify the changes pushed with tags.
They can be seen by choose Container Registry ➤ Services ➤
Repositories. See Figure 6-110.

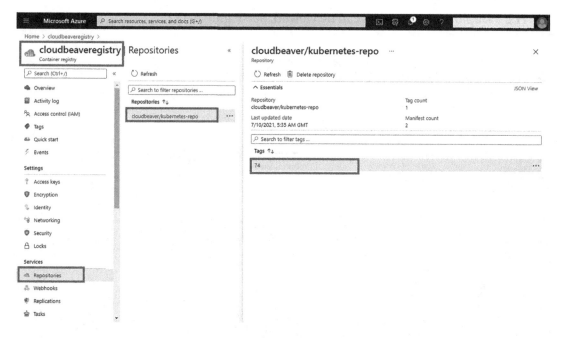

Figure 6-110. *Image detailing Step 110*

111.   Now in the Azure DevOps Portal, under Release, you can see the details
of relevant changes that need to be deployed. See Figure 6-111.

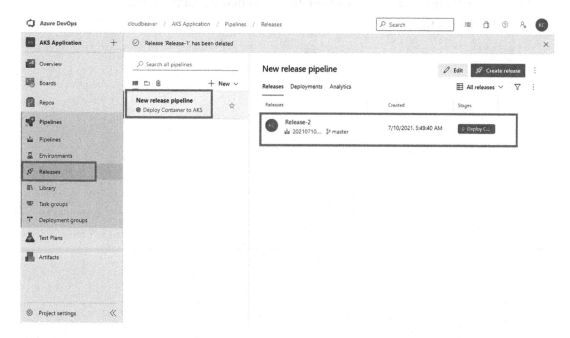

Figure 6-111. *Image detailing Step 111*

112.   Deployment progress can be viewed. See Figure 6-112.

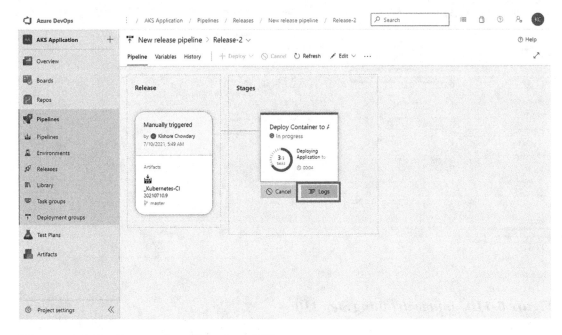

Figure 6-112. *Image detailing Step 112*

113.   By clicking on Logs, you can see the steps being executed. See
Figure 6-113.

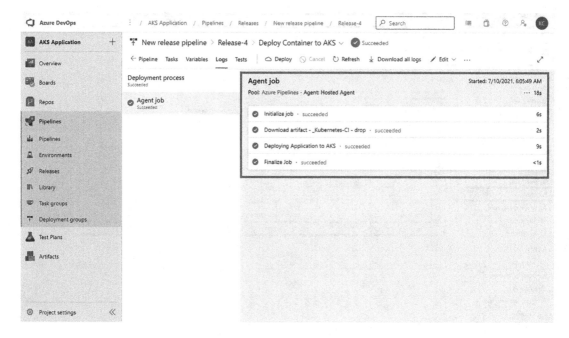

Figure 6-113. *Image detailing Step 113*

114.   From the Azure Portal, choose the Kubernetes Service.
       Under the Kubernetes resources section, select Workloads.
       Under deployments, the latest deployment will be listed. See
       Figure 6-114.

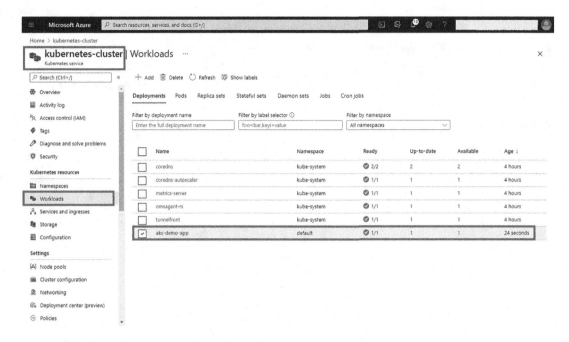

Figure 6-114. *Image detailing Step 114*

115.   Click the listed deployment to view more details. See Figure 6-115.

Figure 6-115. *Image detailing Step 115*

116. Click Overview and then Connect to view the ways to connect the cluster using Azure CLI along with sample commands. Follow the steps shown in Figure 6-116 to connect with AKS using the cloud shell.

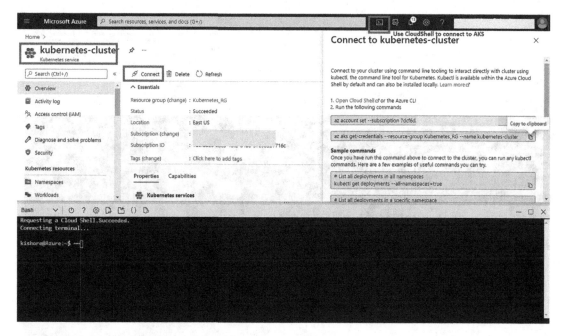

Figure 6-116. *Image detailing Step 116*

117. Copy and enter the commands shown in Figure 6-117. You can host the external IP.

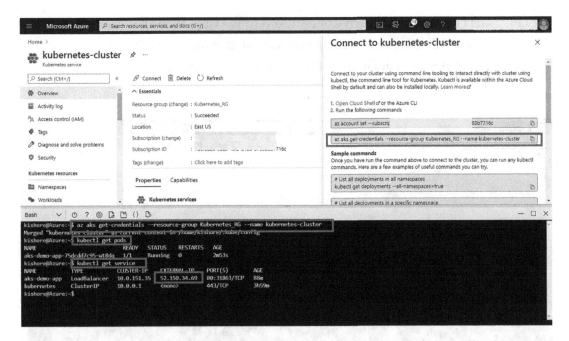

Figure 6-117. *Image detailing Step 117*

118.   Enter the IP in the browser and view the application hosted. See
Figure 6-118.

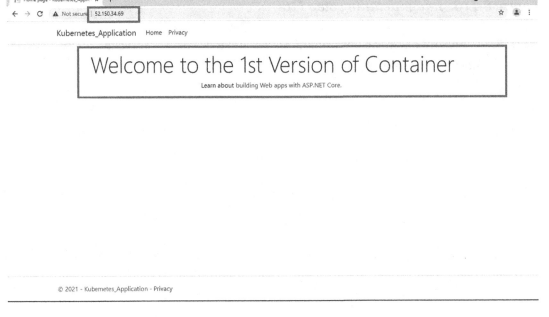

Figure 6-118. *Image detailing Step 118*

119.   Now once validate the CI/CD implementation. See Figure 6-119.

Figure 6-119.   *Image detailing Step 119*

120.   Make small changes to the index file, as shown in Figure 6-120.

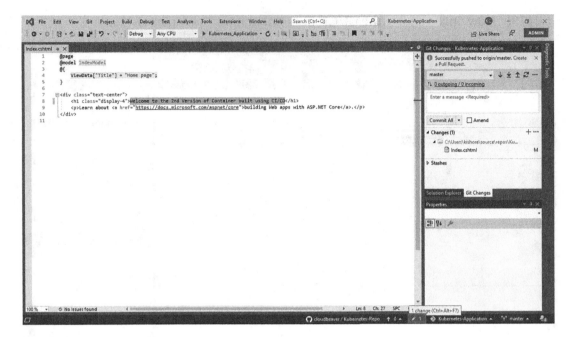

Figure 6-120. *Image detailing Step 120*

121.   Commit and push the new change. See Figure 6-121.

Figure 6-121. *Image detailing Step 121*

122.   Changes can also be seen on GitHub, as shown in Figure 6-122.

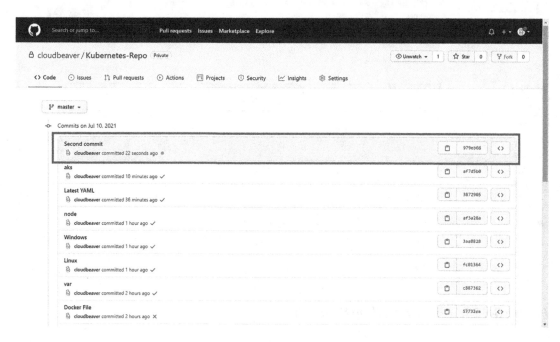

Figure 6-122.   *Image detailing Step 122*

123.   And, of course, you can view the changes in Azure DevOps Portal,
under Pipelines, as shown in Figure 6-123.

Figure 6-123. *Image detailing Step 123*

124.   Under Releases, you can see that the deployment has succeeded. This is because I enabled the continuous deployment trigger. See Figure 6-124.

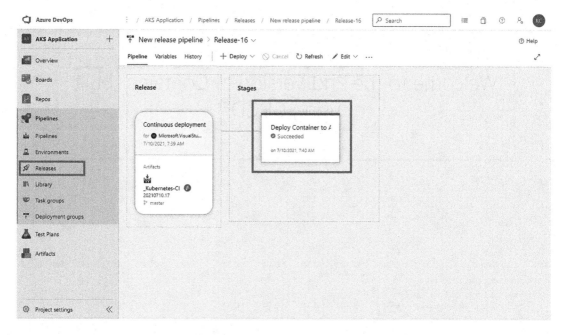

Figure 6-124. *Image detailing Step 124*

125.   In the browser, refresh the page to verify the changes. See Figure 6-125.

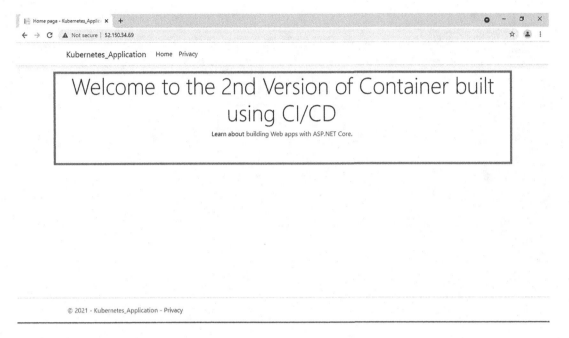

Figure 6-125. *Image detailing Step 125*

And you can see, the application is up and running fine, with the changes made. ☺

Summary

If you followed the steps in this chapter, CI/CD will be successfully implemented in your web application. It's a good idea to follow these steps closely two or three times. Now, as part of the exercise, instead of web application, try to deploy a Web API. You have to change very few steps during the build process. Let me know how it was for you to learn through the adapted step-by-step approach in this chapter and in the other chapters. I hope this book has expedited your learning journey with Azure Kubernetes Services. Thank you for reading this book as part of your learning process. Best of luck and happy Azure learning.

Index

© Kasam Ahmed Shaikh and Shailesh S. Agaskar 2022
K. Ahmed Shaikh and S. S. Agaskar, *Azure Kubernetes Services with Microservices*,
https://doi.org/10.1007/978-1-4842-7809-3

Printed in the United States
by Baker & Taylor Publisher Services

Printed in the United States
by Baker & Taylor Publisher Services